Scott L. Fraser

20 Ways You Lose Money on Your Way to the Stock Market

20 Ways
You Lose
Money

on Your Way
to the
Stock Market

Scott S. Fraser

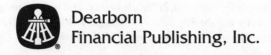
Dearborn
Financial Publishing, Inc.

Managing Editor: Jack Kiburz
Cover Design: DePinto Studios
Interior Design: Lucy Jenkins

Library of Congress Cataloging-in-Publication Data

Fraser, Scott S.
    20 ways you lose money on your way to the stock market / Scott S. Fraser.
       p. cm.
    Includes index.
    ISBN 0-7931-1789-5
    1. Investments—United States.   2. Stocks—United States.
    3. Stock exchanges—United States.   I. Title.
HG4910.F76   1996
332.63′22—dc20   96-288
                                  CIP

ACKNOWLEDGMENTS

Much thanks goes to family and friends who supported my escape from a dark sector of the market jungle. I must acknowledge the national brokerage firm and the investment banking interest that paved the way to my mastery of these 20 ways you lose on your way to the stock market. I am also indebted for the enlightenment from Rick Rule of Global Resource Investments, who showed me how to properly treat and operate in the best interest of the individual investor.

FOREWORD

Through the annals of the U.S. stock market system, the greatest free market economy in the history of the world has been built. Our nation continues to flourish as our industrial indexes move steadily upward, even though during times of social and financial volatility, the principles of our market system have been attacked by small-minded, short-sighted critics. The U.S. stock market system has been resilient in its provision of benefit to the American people.

We owe our wealth as a nation to our publicly traded financial markets, and the rest of the world is indebted to us for the fruits of that wealth. Because of the immense wealth of the United States, we can afford to render our leadership to the nations of the world. We can afford to intervene where the treacherous and the inhumane try to terrorize the weak. We can afford to provide relief where misfortune has landed. These rewards are the results of the global American presence, which has always been financed by the continued strength of the American financial market system.

I am very fortunate to be a part of this market of which I am so proud. A special tribute should be paid to the individual components that form the foundation of this system. These vital components are the millions of individual investors who fuel the markets with their venture capital. Without the millions of individual components, we would have no markets. To the individual, we are also indebted. Through my years of experience with Jefferies and Co. and Global Resource Investments, I can state with complete confidence that there are market institutions that foster the stock market success of the individual investor.

I have often been asked to elaborate on the most important aspect of astute investing. My answer has always involved the attainment of knowledge. I wholeheartedly agree with Mr. Fraser's message that a commitment must be made to understand the basic underlying principles of the stock market. Once the commitment is made, investors can confidently determine whether their particular stocks possess the ability to move up.

—Jeffrey L. Taylor
Principal Officer, The London Taylor Group

CONTENTS

PREFACE

The purpose of this book is to provide you with a mental arsenal of stock market understanding that will protect you from repeating the 20 most common and destructive mistakes in the market. By following the guidelines described in this book carefully, you can be assured that all of your market endeavors will be investments rather than donations.

This book is your opportunity to reverse the trend of predictable and avoidable stock market losses. Regarding each kind of market investment product and activity, this book will reveal the potential for manipulation, why it is being done and which member of the market is the instigator. Once armed with this information, you can put your stock broker, investment firm or fund manager on notice that you are savvy about the most dynamic venture capital market in the world. The informed investor can meet any market participant on even terms and avoid the pitfalls that lie before the realm of investment success.

If investors were on a mission to lose money quickly, the stock market could be an excellent place to do so. This could be clearly seen from my vantage point as a stock broker and a stock promoter. With the phone headset in my ear, the Quotron and the newswire screen in front of me, and my hands on the various promotional devices of phone, fax and marketing slicks, I worked the pulse of the nation's investors. I could see what type of events would drive them out of one position and what type of promotion would pack them into the next. Their emotions, rationale and reactions became completely predictable. Just the right touch of semantics and timing made the promotion the real driving force behind many buying and selling decisions.

These investors were vulnerable to manipulation because they would rather have blind faith in the opportunity of a lifetime being presented to them than learn to detect adverse market forces. As a result, most investors' losses occur during pre-market decisions, *before their money even gets to the stock market.* Apathy and naiveté form the root of the problem. The mistakes are made, repeatedly, when individuals deal with their stock broker, investment firm and personal source of financial market propaganda.

This is not, by any means, an indictment of the stock market. Its place in our free enterprise, capitalist economy is of vital importance. Nor is it an attempt to brand all stockbrokers as dishonest or corrupt. Stockbrokers are truly a product of their environment, and they are becoming the victims of the institutions they serve. My wish is that this text be used as a road map through a mine field—a map that can be used, by the individual investor, to avoid the most common pitfalls.

Who am I? I'm the guy on the other end of the phone, the voice on the other end of the 800 number. I'm the voice behind the ring that interrupts your coffee break or your evening meal. I'm the man with the story to tell you of a unique opportunity that just crossed my desk. I am one of the links connecting individual investors and the broad expanse of the financial markets. If you plan on entering the world of high finance, and on contributing your pile of money to the bigger piles, you had better know who I am and what makes me tick.

I began my financial career as an intern for two of the biggest producing brokers at a branch of a national stock brokerage firm in San Diego. I learned the basics of story telling. I learned to write and read a script that would inspire people to contribute thousands of dollars to an investment idea, with one phone call. After college, I completed a tour as an officer in the U.S. Marine Corps. Somewhere in the months of solitude and the sudden chaos of Desert Storm, I found the inspiration to return to the business. I entered the broker training program for another national stock brokerage firm. My first stint at learning their trade was spent at their headquarters on the Avenue of the Americas and in Weehawken, New Jersey, before being sent to their branch in San Diego.

From day one at the San Diego branch, I knew that the office was destined to fall apart. Due to all sorts of illicit activity, we eventually attracted a wave of government and regulatory agencies that kicked in our door and stormed the office. Countless eyeballs scrutinized the records and many heads rolled. But to this day, the auditors still have not determined what really happened.

I then moved to a firm that specialized in natural resource stocks. The price movement charts looked like electrocardiograms. Most of our positions traded on the frontier exchanges, such as Vancouver, Calgary, Kuala Lumpur and Hong Kong. While there I learned the ways of genuine stock promoters and mastered the manipulation of the emotions of fear and greed.

After a battle of egos with one of the senior partners, I left to make one more stop at an investment banking firm. They specialized in initial public offerings and private placements. Their operating credo was: If you've got a name, a phone and an address, we'll bring your company public, and we'll convince the public to pay for it.

Then it happened. I was more surprised than anybody. Right after a typical phone call with a long-time client, I became ethically burned out. After convincing my 65-year-old customer that a particular initial public offering had all the characteristics of a real winner, I felt a rush of anxiety come over me. All the pitches, the manipulations, the contrived senses of urgency, the buzz words and the tricks of the trade came back to me at once. As of that moment I couldn't do it any longer. I leaned into my partner's office and told him that I was done. He was a good man but still indoctrinated. My comments didn't even register. I left him a note.

Now I'm here to share my experiences with you. My message is for the benefit of the individual investor. This analysis of the 20 ways you lose money on your way to the stock market should lead to the development of your personal criteria for what to avoid. It is not an investment formula based on fundamental or technical market theory. The reasons I give for avoidance are not based on my opinion of possible index fluctuations or where I think the next hot industry sector will be. The information that I am going to give you comes from my experience as a broker and a promoter. You need to be aware of how I made my living. It will help you from being taken advantage of by the system. There is already enough market risk that cannot be circumvented. To get your funds to the market, you must navigate through a barrage of pitches, hype and "expert" advice. The following information should help. Good luck.

CHAPTER 1

Coming to Terms with the Stock Market

A Few Basics

The appearance of the stock market as an alien and unfathomable entity is by deliberate design. Upon my graduation from initial broker training, the president of the investment brokerage firm proclaimed that my class now knew more than 99.8 percent of the population about the stock market. I'd like to close the gap by sharing a few of the basic lesson we learned with you.

The first is paramount: The only way for your particular stock price to go up is by more people buying the stock after you than bought before you. Current buy orders must overwhelm sell orders. The mere fact that a company has a solid balance sheet, impressive product line, and a dominant market share, does not increase its share price. The stock price will move up when its current buying volume begins to increase. As more attention of buyers is brought to the stock, the sellers demand a higher price.

Brokerage firms and promoters have mastered this concept. They first purchase a large block of shares of a certain stock. Then they start their own internal propaganda machine via their brokers, research reports and news releases. The presentation of the stock attracts buying interest. The brokerage house sells its position as the individual clients bid the price up. During this time, the stock, which normally trades at approximately 50,000 shares a day, can temporarily increase five to ten times in volume. When the volume returns to normal, the price usually comes back down as well. This phenomenon is due to the herd mentality of individual investors. I will address this subject later as one of the ways you lose money on your way to the stock market.

A second related lesson explains the causes behind quick, drastic movements in a stock price. Sharp price fluctuations are the product of panic buying or panic selling. This panic is driven by the emotion of fear or greed. Its effects on the share price are usually temporary. This short-lived stampede is often started by someone with a vested interest. This person is usually well read in the ways of lemmings.

The third lesson is to realize who you are in the financial market. Investors are those who bring piles of money to the marketplace. These investors fall under two categories, either institutional or individual retail investors. If you call or are called by a brokerage investment firm, and your broker is a registered representative, consider yourself an individual retail investor. Unless your account is valued at somewhere above six digits, you fall under this category. The institutional investor is usually a large company or fund of substantial monetary means and enjoys preferential treatment over the individual.

The individual investors need to become informed, for they are not granted the advantages of their institutional counterparts. At national brokerage or wirehouses, the institutional accounts are serviced at the headquarters, usually in New York. The individual accounts are handled by the branch offices throughout the country. The relationship between the institutional accounts and the individual accounts is simple: When necessary, the national firm will sacrifice the individual client for the benefit of the institutional client. Consider the following example.

The Stock Switch Scam

The Boston City Employees Pension Fund is an institutional account. The stock portfolio currently holds two million shares of U.S. Surgical. The analyst feels it's time to sell the entire position. If the headquarters begins to sell this large amount of the stock directly into the market, the price will begin to plummet. Their institutional client will see a substantial decrease in the net proceeds from the sell. The preferred method of handling this situation is to have the individual investors lend a helping hand. At the headquarters, there is a microphone that transmits into the squawk boxes in the branch offices throughout the country. The analyst speaks into the microphone and begins to tout the enormous opportunity that exists in the stock of U.S. Surgical. The transmission goes out in the morning, just before the market opens.

By mid-morning, the branch managers hold a quick meeting concerning the hot new buy recommendation. They inevitably mention that this is one of the strongest stock plays they've seen in awhile. The manager's closing comment is that there's an extra ⅛, or .125 cents per share bonus for the broker, for each share their client buys. To further support the operation, the corporate printing office is mailing off the current recommendation list with U.S. Surgical as the hot addition.

Across the branch offices, there is a flurry of activity involving thousands of phone numbers being dialed, thousands of stories being told and thousands of buy orders being accumulated. These orders are parked on the institutional trader's desk until just before the close of the market day. The day's total of buy orders is for 750,000 shares. The trader crosses or arranges for the sale and purchase of that exact share amount, from the institutional account into the various individual investors' accounts, and reports the volume of the transaction to the proper exchange.

This process continues for the next few trading days until the entire two million shares has been crossed. For the brokerage firm, the benefit is threefold. The first benefit is the spread. If the stock is trading at 40⅛ by 40⅝, the 50 cents in-between goes to the house. (The lower number is the bid or how much you receive if you are selling; the higher number is the ask or how much you have to pay if you are buying.)

The second benefit is their share of any commissions charged to the individual investors on the buy side. Normally, a brokerage firm isn't allowed to charge a commission and take the spread, but you'd be amazed at how creative it can get.

Third, the investment brokerage firm has done its best to protect the interests of the institutional client. These are the clients who bring the brokerage firm its real profits, due to the large amounts of assets and bulk trading involved. The individual investor, on the other hand, is left to hold the position and now carries all the market risk. This is an example of how the national brokerage firm took the supply from its institutional account and created the demand within its retail accounts, to service its own best interests.

Let the Investor Beware

Your perception of the stock market should be cynical, at best. Remember that everyone's got an angle. Whether good or bad, there are ulterior motives behind every recommendation. Individual investors need to know where they are situated in the cycle, during any particular run in a stock price. To be successful, it takes more than just an understanding of market fundamentals. True investor savvy requires a clear perception of the techniques used by those who derive their livelihood from the market. A great deal of money can be made in this arena and there are many talented brokers, but let's consider the market for what it really is: the world's most dynamic venture capital market surrounded by pitfalls and traps aimed at the unwary individual investor.

The majority of investors consistently make the same basic mistakes. As we proceed to detail the 20 ways you lose money on your way to the stock market, consider your own investment formula. Most individual investors would deny that their objective is to lose money in the stock market investments. Compare how closely your own investment formula matches the following techniques.

CHAPTER 2

Successful Avoidance and Profitable Exploitation of the Herd Mentality

The Ways You Lose: 1

In the Stock Market, There's Insecurity in Numbers

Social animals traditionally believe security can be found in large numbers. The wildebeest knows he would not get very far, if he decided to make his trek across the Serengeti in solo formation. The pragmatic quality of group participation has been proven throughout the food chain. Imagine the tough sell for the original lemming, who tried to convince his peers of the benefits to cliff jumping. This early pioneer of persuasion must have won numerous converts to the idea of altruistic self-sacrifice, beforehand. Then he kicked off the first-ever mad dash over the edge. He knew once the primary group started to move in one direction, natural instinct would compel the onlookers to follow. This lemming is still honored throughout the world at his species annual picnic and ledge runs.

Whatever the function or objective, the progress of any endeavor is usually propelled by increased group participation. Humankind adapted this concept quite efficiently while developing its own societies. Humans developed the same herd mentality as existed among the wild animals. For as long as humans have embraced the herd mentality to feel secure, there have been select humans who have been able to exploit it for profit.

The desire to do like everyone else is the foundation of the herd mentality. Regardless of the wisdom related to the particular popular movement, it is safe to go with the majority. Fewer people can ridicule you when you're wrong.

The targets of the herd mentality continually change. If the herd is not currently headed your way, just hold tight because it will get to you eventually. An excellent example can be found in the infinite number of styles in society. Every functioning sector in society adheres to a definitive style, which currently exists somewhere in the spectrum between obscurity and popularity. The position within the spectrum will change quickly if the herd charges in a new direction. The power of mass popular movement sparks a drastic metamorphosis. The style is elevated into becoming a fashion. This elevated public profile expands the fashion into a substantial trend. As the herd completely inhabits into the former style, the result is social saturation. A new target is located on the horizon. With the same quickness of its arrival, the herd hastens its departure to the next feeding ground.

Beyond the inherent costs of a product's manufacture, the herd is also responsible for dictating the current value of any product. Depending on the degree of the herd's movements, the effects on value can be sudden and devastating. Property prices are subject to such judgment from an external entity. The only reason a home in the coastal strip of southern California is much more expensive than a similar home in Kansas City is because the herd has deemed it so. Both homes can be built with the same care and quality. But if more people are trying to buy homes in southern California, the prices will be multiples higher than the homes in the plains states.

The preferences of the herd have granted the properties of southern California the bulk of its perceived value. Beyond the material costs, the popular desire for these properties was what inflated prices. However, the early 1990s demonstrated how quickly this major part of a property's price can evaporate. California coastal cities, like Del Mar, experienced property value peaks sometime in 1989. Within 24 months, some unfortunate homeowners endured losses near 50 percent of original property assessments. This painful lesson is a tribute to two basic concepts:

1. The bulk of any item's market value is based on intangibles, such as the currently perceived supply and demand.

2. The law of gravity eventually applies to any running market sector.

The Great Herds of the Stock Market

The stock market depends on the herd mentality for the movement across its many sectors. The current price of a stock reflects what the market will bear, for the moment. External events drive a stock to bear a higher or lower price. Whether these external events naturally occur or are fabricated, a substantial response from the herd is required if the share price is to be effected. This premise supports a basic principle of the stock market:

The operational quality of a particular company is not directly related to the performance of its stock. The degree and direction of any share price movement is determined by the amount of buying or selling pressure, that can be channeled toward the stock. The herd's buying and selling power is used as the muscle behind the movement. This muscle is controlled by forces outside the minds of individual herd members. Thus, buying interest or selling interest must overwhelm the other side of a stock's market, before movement can occur.

A feature story on the cover of national financial news magazines, a televised commentary by a well-known analyst or a barrage of broker phone calls carries the influence to the investing public. The message dictates either buying or selling and where it should occur. The public's response comes in an incremental fashion. There are individuals who respond to the influence and act immediately. Others wait until they are convinced by the movement of the featured stock or by one of their office associates.

The featured stock story and recommendation becomes a self-fulfilling prophecy. If the public is effectively told a certain stock or stock sector should be purchased because of a pending price surge, then it will probably happen. As the first group of individuals follow the buy influence, the stock will begin to move on higher volume. If the influence is well received, the buying response will continue. Those who were observing the movement will be stirred to buy and prolong the upward trend.

The investing public responds to influence pertaining to individual stocks more quickly than to influence pertaining to broader stock sectors. They will react quickly to prevent missing any boat of opportunity. Stock charts characteristically display periods of drastic price fluctuations.

The people who follow the influence featuring sectors of the stock market, are primarily mutual fund investors. These people are traditionally very slow to react. They often need to be told numerous times why they should buy or sell. This necessary repetitiveness often involves all the available forms of investment influence. Fear and greed do not have a tremendous effect on mutual fund investors. The mutual fund investor is merely striving for an atmosphere of comfort. For them, it is not necessary to actually make money; they just don't want to incur too much risk. Their response time, to act on influence, is incrementally delayed. When the market media begin to tout the strength of a certain stock market sector, there is usually a substantial proliferation of new mutual funds in that sector, over the next year.

The driving forces that influence the public by featuring specific areas of the stock market and other forms of persuasion can conjure a powerful reaction. With this ability, it is possible to make a stock go up or down by merely saying that it will. If the masses did not instinctively follow a herd mentality, such manipulation would never be possible. For those who receive and respond to the buy and sell influence, an extremely difficult task is at hand. The individual investor must try to determine the angle of the person or medium being influential and at what point this temporarily self-fulfilling prophecy will reverse itself.

For Some, the Manual of the Herd Mentality Is Required Reading

Complete comprehension of the herd mentality is essential for those who make their living within the stock market. Whether the forces that attract attention to a particular stock are natural or created, market professionals know this represents the demand into which an established supply of the stock can be fed.

When many individual investors are rushing to buy a specific stock in higher than normal volumes, there must be an entity supplying the stock on the sell side of these transactions. This entity is often an institution that had a sizable position in the specific stock. As the buying interest grows, so does the selling interest of the institution, which continues to feed its shares into a market moving upward. An objective observer might wonder why the ostensibly savvy institution would want to sell its stock during this time of strength.

It is because this market entity truly understands the risk, and potential peril, involved in holding any stock position. A stock is only as valuable as the price the current market will bear. If the investing public is motivated to buy a stock that is currently heavy in a firm's inventory the firm will take the short-term profits and let the public endure the risk of holding an intangible, for the long-term. This panic buying is usually followed by panic selling, which can allow the institution to eventually buy back the stock at a lower price.

The outstanding supply of any company's stock is relatively steady. The fluctuating factor is the public's current interest in buying or selling that stock. The direction of the interest depends on what the masses are being told or how world events are being interpreted for them. For those who toil within the market, the plan is simple: If natural events drive the herd's buying interest to a position in the inventory, take the short-term profits. If the herd's interest doesn't come naturally to the stocks in the inventory, create the necessary attraction.

The Herd Mentality Can Be a Profitable Tool for the Individual Investor

The herd mentality can be used for fun and profit. At the very least, it can be used by the individual investor to avoid further self-victimization. A change in thought is required rather than any specific action.

First, step back and take an objective, unemotional look at what is involved in a stock transaction. There are three basic parties engaging in a specific action, each with its own ramifications. One side is the seller. The other side is a buyer. These two sides are joined in the middle by a brokerage/exchange entity.

The selling side has become convinced the time is right to unload its position. This side does not want to sell its shares into a tumbling market. If this selling side is fortunate, it holds its shares in an institutional account. The account is handled by an investment firm that will unload the stock onto its retail client base so the share price will not be substantially hammered from mass selling pressure. The optimum scenario for the seller is to unload its position into a sudden demand for the stock. The second best scenario occurs when this sudden demand doesn't appear, but the seller has the means to create demand and feed its shares into it.

The exchange entity, in the middle, does not have to be convinced of anything. This uniting force of buyers and sellers is not concerned with investment decisions. Activity is the only important matter, because each share of every transaction pays a little bit to those in the middle. The direction of the stock is of minor relevance. It is the volume of shares traded that pulls the profit heartstrings of the people between the buy and the sell.

The buy side harbors the opposite sentiment of the selling side. The buy side has come to the conclusion that now is the time to purchase the stock. The buyer could be a market institution that intends to establish a substantial position through well-planned increments. The stock is purchased in certain blocks, over a duration of market days, so the share price doesn't run up due to an overwhelming dose of buying pressure. The market institution does not want to pay more than is necessary to establish its position, especially if it plans to employ its means of promotion to run the share price up, at a later time. The buyer could be an institutional account that is being afforded a privileged buying environment from its firm. However, if the buyer is an individual investor, she is usually acting under the influence of a biased or an ignorant information source. The individual buyer is making her purchase, during an upward trend, from a much larger seller. This seller is often the same entity that issued the convincing promotion. If the individual buyer is not being directly influenced, she is usually acting on second-hand information from a novice associate.

As an individual investor, you should focus on the origins of your purchase interest. You must consider the possible angles and ulterior motives of the source. You should recite the supporting factors of your potential purchase aloud, to determine if they sound reasonable, and avoid supporting the best possible scenarios for the seller.

Essential Underlying Principles for Understanding the Herd Mentality

After an objective view of the stock transaction, as an enlightened investor you should accept the intangibility of stocks in general. Unlike bonds and other debt instruments, stocks are not asset-backed. A stock purchase does represent ownership in a company, but share price reflects the market's present perception of the underlying company's worth and future potential. This perception can be modified and manipulated by natural or created forces.

Acknowledge and respect the law of gravity within the stock market. In this realm, where a high degree of probability is the highest possible level of certainty, most stocks spend their market days running up and back down. Thus, it is unlikely that a boat of opportunity will ever be missed, for good.

You should make a final mental check before purchasing a stock. You should be confident your decision is emotionally, philosophically, practically and strategically sound. At least you should be able to say you are buying the stock due to sound reasoning, not just because someone told you to.

A decent tip is to consider last year's model. A stock that has been promoted and touted to lofty heights in the past will probably receive the same attention again. The smart buying will be done before the herd is called back. Stock buys should be made in calm times or after a down-turn and following a calculated decision. If a stock's price, trading volume, and promotional activity are currently running upward, then it probably isn't the best time to buy the shares.

The Majority of Investors Will Always Embrace the Herd Mentality

There will always be blind adherence to the blatant and subliminal influence issued by the dwellers of the market jungle. There will always be individual investors who only buy what is presented to them. That is why so many people buy mutual funds. They have been told, for so long, it's just the thing to do. These people are rarely clear on their objective or justification for the fund purchase, but there does seem to be a feeling of comfort. They are simply bombarded with constant buy signals, and they respond with their checkbooks in a herdlike fashion. It is the same for specific stocks that are featured in publications, television and telephone presentations.

Individuals who embrace the security in numbers concept will continue to invest with the rest of the herd. By perpetuating the herd mentality, these investors will continue to serve their institutional masters on the other side of the transaction. The herd members will all be able to console each other, after they participate in such mass premarket decisions relating to the first way you lose money.

WAY #1: *The herd mentality: Buy the stocks that are currently popular.* A stock or an entire market sector currently being featured by the financial news media and propaganda signals a powerful endorsement. A stock that has been moving up in price and trading volume is already a proven winner. Just think of those fools who are selling their shares of this fine upwardly mobile stock. Let's all join hands and keep buying that stock together; who knows how long we can keep this upward momentum going? Millions of lemmings can't be all wrong.

CHAPTER 3

Circumventing the Inherent Traps of Initial Public Offerings

The Ways You Lose: 2, 3 and 4

What Is an IPO?

Initial public offerings are affectionately referred to as IPOs. When a private company (profitable or not) decides to become a public company, it initiates an initial offering to the public of its common stock. The company will do this through the investment banking division of one or more brokerage firms. This is a profitable arrangement for both parties. The company receives a tremendous amount of nondebt capital the day its shares are initially purchased and begin trading on the market. The brokerage firms that place the shares with the investors receive a percentage of the price at which the shares initially trade, plus the customary underwriting fee. The company does not mind paying this fee because they pass the cost on to the shareholders. The firm also receives a large amount of warrants that allow the stock to be purchased in the future, well below the current market price. A typical relationship between a company desiring to go public and an investment banking interest retained to do the underwriting is reflected in the following example.

A new company named Del Mar Beverages sells a flavored drink that uses desalinated ocean water. The company is currently distributing its product to vendors on a temporary promotional basis. Its first objective is to gain recognition, establish a distribution network and begin to gain a market share of the beverage sector. Unfortunately, these types of endeavors cost quite a bit of money, and this fledgling company has no current earnings. It does have accumulating debt whose deadlines are quickly approaching. What Del Mar Beverages needs is an infusion of venture capital that incurs no repayment obligation and some free advertising to accompany the deal. Thus in a flash of brilliance, the board of directors decides to take the company public.

Del Mar Beverages begins to solicit various investment banking interests to find institutions to bring the company's shares to the public. The board of directors hits the street touting the conceptual greatness of their company. Their road show involves stops at as many brokerage houses as possible. Your first clue that something is amiss should be this: When a private company has a solid balance sheet, a sound operation, and is worthy of consideration, the investment banking world usually knocks on its door with offers to take it public.

Eventually a few securities firms agree to conduct the initial public offering of Del Mar Beverages. Between the company and the investment banking division of the securities firm, there are a few decisions that need to be made. How much capital needs to be raised? What is its share price? What will be the stated purpose for utilizing the money, and what percentage of the initially traded share price will go to the investment bank when the stock hits the market? The big question is how many warrants is the securities firm entitled to and how many shares will they be able to buy, at a later date, well under the current market price? This is how these firms load up on cheap stock, promote it and then sell it to you sometime down the road.

Your second clue that there are problems lies in the stated purpose for how the company will utilize the money. When considering investments, a good reason for a company to raise capital by going public would be that it already has a profitable product with a growing market share, but its manufacturing facilities are limited. The capital would be used to increase production capacity, thus increasing profitability.

A bad reason for a company to raise capital by going public is to create a distribution network for its product. If it doesn't have a network already in place, it doesn't have profits. If its product is an existing idea, it doesn't have any special appeal. Chances are the company, much like the investment, will be a promise that is never fulfilled.

The securities firm tries to determine what the current market will bear. It considers the appeal of the Del Mar Beverages concept. How much capital can it raise based on the drinking water idea? Is the industry sector already diluted? How can it get its brokers to sell the stock to their clients? These are all considerations.

The firm will also receive an underwriting fee during this planning process. It is important that the initial public offering is carefully planned. A realistic and acceptable share price needs to be set. The promotion needs to be well-timed and thorough. The incentives need to be strong enough to win the cooperation of the brokers. It is only when the company's shares are fully placed, and the stock becomes publicly traded, that this windfall of profits can be realized.

The planning is soon completed and the strategy is set. The investment banking side presents the retail securities side with the following package:

The initial public offering of Del Mar Beverages will be for 10 million shares at $5 per share. The stock is scheduled to begin trading on the exchange in 60 days. The yield to the broker is 8 percent for total shares placed with the clients. A broker that places 100,000 shares of the IPO receives gross commissions of $40,000. His net on those commissions is between 30 and 70 percent, depending on his payout arrangement.

The promotion team is standing by with enormous amounts of marketing collateral ready for circulation by mail, fax, news release and seminars. It is crucial that the offering period be successful. If the firm can get the shares placed and the stock begins trading, the gross profits will be $0.85 per share or $8.5 million, plus the value of the stock purchase warrants. It is also important that the firm prove its prowess to other companies who might go public in the future.

A company wants its investment bank to create a stable market capitalization, especially when its stock initially starts trading. The investment firm will try to keep the stock price stable, if not up, for at least the first few weeks of trading. To do this, it will charge the brokers with a penalty bid. This means that if a client sells the stock within the first 30 days of trading, the broker will lose his original commission. Thus the broker will do anything it takes to keep the client in the stock. The firm will also maintain buying pressure in the stock, after the IPO, by giving special incentives to the brokers and continuing the promotion. All this is to secure future initial public offering business.

Pitching the IPO Stock

Now the offering period is officially started, and the brokers take the stage. Their headsets are turned on, and the scripted phone pitches are taped on the wall in front of them. The piles of material stacked around the office include offering prospectuses and promotional literature, waiting to be stuffed into envelopes. The biggest stack of all is the lead list. This enormous computer printout contains the names, numbers and addresses of all the individuals who have ever had even remote contact with the financial world. There are hundreds of thousands of names, from every category, instantly available to the brokers preparing for a pitch session. It is very simple. All the broker needs to know is the product, the payout, the pitch and about a million numbers to call. It's merely a numbers game. Even the newest and most inexperienced broker can place her allotment of the initial public offering, if she dials enough numbers.

On the office walls hang number boards that display the current total of shares placed for the present offering. The totals are updated on an hourly basis. With a frightening similarity to a warped, charity telethon atmosphere, whenever a big order ticket is dropped, the bell sounds, and its impact is immediately reflected in the display total. Oohs and aahs resound from the rookies in the bull pen.

During this offering period, the broker has three basic sources to which he can place the shares. His former clients, his current clients and prospective clients from referrals comprise the list. There is tremendous buying power in these three sources as a whole. Each group has a different history and perception of the market. Thus, each group needs to be handled differently.

Handling a Former Client

The former clients are those who were very active for about one year. They had probably opened their account after a windfall had yielded money to invest. Perhaps the account was opened after the client's previous brokerage firm mistreated him. Regardless of its origin, the account is opened and is allocated in the standard manner. One quarter of the funds are placed into a currently traded recommendation. No doubt it is a stock from the firm's inventory, which the firm pushes as "chock full of profit potential." The second quarter of the funds are put into whatever initial public offering the firm has pending.

The third quarter of the funds are used to purchase an unsubstantiated stock, based on hearsay information. A naive investor may have heard of a stock through an associate who talks with a company's investor relations people once a week and says it's going global. The client then requests that the broker invest in the stock and the broker happily complies.

The fourth quarter of the money is temporarily kept in cash. The broker wants the funds to be available in case of the sudden appearance of a tremendous opportunity with inherent incentive. Possible opportunities include a particular stock that has become heavy in the firm's inventory, or the stock of a company that is offering cooperative brokers a back door contribution to their retirement fund. These funds could always be used as supportive purchasing power for the free-falling IPO during the first week of trading. This portion of the account's assets will not stay in cash form for long. Every broker knows that if the cash is not utilized in a certain period of time, the client might remember it is her money and want to spend it elsewhere.

The broker actively trades the account as the weeks pass. The theme is that idle money is lost money. All or portions of certain positions are sold to create the funds to buy the next stock position. The broker justifies the trades, explaining that the original assessment of a company was incorrect or the market conditions of a sector have changed or perhaps that the presence of an 8 percent profit in seven days should be taken off the table. Thus, it's necessary to change strategies. The trades are executed and the commissions are made.

Soon, the broker purchases option contracts and requests that more funds be deposited into the account. When all the available funds have been invested, the broker introduces the idea of using margin to the client. Converting an account to a margin arrangement allows the client to borrow between 50 and 80 percent of the account's market value to make more investments. The client instantly increases her buying power tremendously, at a time when the broker was predicting the strongest bull market of all time. Margin is touted as a wonderful opportunity to make bigger trades, realize potentially bigger profits and pay bigger commissions just like those big time, sophisticated, professional investors.

Over the next few months, the client is never quite sure how the account is doing. The barrage of encrypted statements, trade confirmations and verbal confusion balls tossed by the broker have made it impossible to see the bottom line. Even the most obvious drop in a stock's trading price is explained away with the proper broker response.

Unfortunately, even the thickest cloud of confusion dissipates eventually. One day, at three o'clock in the morning, the client sits up in bed and begins to ponder her stock account. She goes downstairs and pulls out all the monthly statements, trade confirmations and notes from the conversations with her broker, if she was smart enough to keep them. After putting her mind and calculator to work, that once evasive bottom line begins to shine like a beacon of reality. At best, her findings reflect that the retail brokerage firm's guidance had an overall neutral effect on the value of her portfolio. It's more likely that the findings indicate, as the account activity increased and the piles of money moved around often, the value of the total pile continued to decrease.

The trading patterns and positions show the account adhered to no particular strategy or strived for any specific goal. The client realizes her apathy and unconditional acceptance of past events has decreased her net asset value considerably. It becomes apparent that having your money lost by a trained, registered professional isn't all it's cracked up to be. With stern resolve, she vows to close the account the next day and transfer it to a discount firm. At first this move will make her feel better, but soon she will be in the same position, because she will most likely make the same mistakes again and even some new ones of a different caliber.

Now, as the broker dials his former client's number, he thinks about what he will say. The client answers the phone and hears that old familiar voice from the investment firm of Dewey, Cheatham and Howe. The broker preludes his pitch with all the skills he mastered at broker charm school. "Ms. Magilicutty, I realize that I'm probably not anywhere near the top of your list of favorite people, but I just wanted three minutes of your time to explain a few things."

Once she agrees to grant the three minutes, the broker has a decent chance of bringing her back into the loop.

The broker continues,"We both know that the account did not do too well over the last 12 months. Although our strategy was sound, the results were just not there. Perhaps we were unrealistic, maybe 12 months was simply too short of a time frame to reach our goals. We both know that Microsoft wasn't built in a day."

The broker waits for any agreeable response, even a grunt. With not much time to spare, the broker moves to the next step.

"But hey, the past is done and we can only be concerned with what is next. Which is exactly why I wanted to call you first. Our investment banking division is part of the underwriting group bringing Del Mar Beverages public. At any moment, the offering will become oversubscribed, which means that all the shares are sold before they start trading. However, since my overall performance has been very good here at the firm, I will receive an allocation of shares to make available to my preferred clients. And with the pending oversubscription, heavy institutional interest in the company's stock and a dynamic product, I don't even want to guess how far the buying power of a hungry public will drive the share price when trading begins. So I must be very selective when putting my allocation in certain accounts. You and I have some history together. I have always valued the business we have done and I would like to reestablish our relationship. So I will commit part of my allocation to you. I don't know how many shares I will receive, but you will have a part of them if you will allow us to start again on the right foot."

I know this sounds like a cheesy used car ad, but you'd would be amazed at the success ratio. A client who has taken some hits in her account and has been slightly abused is searching for a ray of hope. A good story, with plenty of promise, can provide that ray. Many of the former clients will feel they deserve some special consideration after all they have been through. Thus, a number of the former clients come back on board. A broker never forgets this source of business.

Current Clients: An Easy Sell

The second source for placing the shares are the current clients. The approach for this group is fairly simple. These people are still in the midst of the cloud of confusion that the former clients had to pass through. For an account with current positions, a cash balance or some buying power still remaining from the margin agreement, it should take the broker only one phone call to place a portion of the shares. The typical pitch is known as the assumed close.

"Hello Mrs. Anderson, I've got some great news. Your account just received approval, from the investment banking department, for an allotment of shares on the initial public offering of Del Mar Beverages." The broker will then pause to see just how ecstatic the client is about the news.

"I was a tad concerned at first because there has been such a high demand for the offering. Usually a hot deal is oversubscribed and it only goes to institutional investors, but I called in a favor so we'll be able to participate. I've already pulled the funds out of our Ascoe Mines position, since their drill results will be delayed a few months and the money is in place for the IPO."

After this typical assumed close, if the broker does not hear any protest to what he told the client has already happened, he goes ahead and sells the mining stock and buys the shares of the initial public offering.

New Clients: New Blood

New clients are the third source of business for an IPO. These are primarily referrals from current clients or receptive names off the prospect list. New accounts are crucial because as parts of a broker's client book drop off, new blood must be obtained as replacements. When the broker calls the referral, given to him by his client, the approach is simple.

"Well, Bill called me and said that he'd like to see you get some of these new shares of Del Mar Beverages. Now the shares are completely placed, but it is important to me to keep Bill as a client, so I will do what is necessary to get a block of the stock for you."

The method for receptive individuals called off the prospect list is similar. A broker might state the following: "Mr. Turner, with all the positive aspects surrounding this IPO of Del Mar Beverages, I am going to make a lot of friends in the accounts that get the shares. And to expand my business, it is very important to start new accounts, and to start the accounts with a winner, Mr. Turner, I want your brokerage business. I will get you a block of these IPO shares. Of course I will not charge you a commission on the way into the position and if we have not made a profit after the first thirty days, I will not charge a commission on the way out."

Remember that the broker must keep the client in the stock for at least the first 30 days of trading in order to receive his commission from the investment bank.

The broker has now compiled numerous positive responses from all three sources. He must decide what is the maximum number of shares to offer each client and still make it all seem like a rare, hot deal. This decision must be made on an individual basis. Using his records and notes, the broker must determine the average principle value of the clients' previous positions. If the average initial position value is $10,000, the allocation pitch goes as follows: "With the anticipated oversubscription for Del Mar Beverages, we have to high-ball our request for shares. At the $5 initial public offering price, we'll put in for 5,000 shares. Now realistically we won't even get half of that, but by going high on our request, we should get at least 2,500 shares."

The broker is staying within the client's average position value range. He then adds one more step to the allocation pitch. "Now granted, we'll get less than half of our original share request, but we'll take the rest of our unused funds and buy more shares as soon as trading opens."

This addition is necessary for many brokers, because they are often required by their firm to furnish a certain percentage of clients who buy IPO shares before trading begins, and a certain percentage of clients who buy when trading begins in the after market. If not, his commissions are reduced or reversed. The broker can offer the second purchase of shares, in the active market, without a commission. His firm made the initial public offering and will also make a market in the stock. Thus, the broker will be paid out of the spread, or the difference between the lower number and the higher number in the quoted price.

The Paradox of the IPO Investment

At this point, I need to convey the third and most important tip concerning IPOs: If a broker can get you a large number of shares of an initial public offering, in general and in relation to your account value, you should avoid taking a position.

When a solid company is being taken public and the deal really is hot, oversubscribed and has actually attracted a tremendous amount of buying power that will drive up the stock price on the opening, almost all the shares will go to the investment firms' institutional clients. If any part of the offering does go to the individual investor, it will be a very small amount. The brokers will only be able to allocate tiny blocks of shares as mere tokens of appreciation to their oldest, most active and highest net worth accounts. Why would a broker give you the few precious shares of the good offerings, unless yours is the type of account that can really boost his earnings? Even for the preferred or A accounts, the share amounts granted of the quality offerings are so low that any gains are nominal.

From my perspective as a broker, there are no absolutes in any investment, especially IPOs. There are success and failure percentages that I have observed to be very predictable over the years. There will always be exceptions to any rule or theory. Most of the time, individual investors are best advised to avoid any initial public offering that is available to them in any amount more than nominal. Remember the investment firm devotes their loyalty to the company that they are taking public. It is the underwriting fees, percentages of initial share price and the stock warrants that bring the real profits. To obtain those profits, the investment firm must convince the individual investors to provide the buying power. The broker can always allocate IPO shares without a commission, because he is paid a sales credit from the firm. Buying or selling the shares in the active market can also be done without a commission, because the firm is now a market maker and pays the broker from the spread.

The brokers manipulate investors' emotions by touting amazing IPO success stories, such as Snapple or Boston Chicken, and then compare them to whatever lesser company their firm is trying to bring public. Then the investors let their greed get the best of them. Yet, typical initial public offerings are very numerous and are truly worth a dime a dozen. In addition, on average, between 20 and 25 percent of the stock's initial market price goes to pay underwriting fees, sales credits and the promoter bill. And they say that they don't charge a commission.

The Impending Peril of the Opening Day of Trading

Like a procession of zombies moving towards a crypt, the spell-bound investors line up with their newly purchased shares before the first day of trading. Ten million shares, at $5 per share, have been placed with investors around the nation. At 9:30 E.S.T. the bell rings and the market opens. Del Mar Beverages is on the screen with a brand new shiny stock symbol. The opening price quote is 5 bid and 5⅛ ask. This is the point where the money actually changes hands. The ten million new shares of stock become the possession of the investors, and their $50 million moves away from them. A good portion of the money does go to Del Mar Beverages, so perhaps the company can go forward and do great things. The underwriters take about a dollar per share for the investment bank, the promoters and the brokers. Thus, the part of the share price that could even possibly be backed by the net asset value, per share, of the company is somewhere well below the $5 initial offering price. And again they say that they don't charge a commission.

The first day of trading continues, and the trading volume steadily increases. There must be increased buying demand of Del Mar Beverages in the stock's first few weeks of trading, if the price is going to go up. At the very least, more people must want to buy these shares than want to sell them to maintain the current price. Regardless of the broker's valiant efforts, there will be a good number of clients who want to sell the stock right away, if there is no gain or merely a nominal price increase on the opening. The buying side of the initial volume is from the prearranged market orders and any new orders right after the opening. This maintains the stock's price in its early stages. Once the stock is public and trading, the investment firm becomes the market maker. It will continue to make money regardless of the price at which the stock trades, because the firm, its traders and its brokers supply the buyer and the seller and take the spread between the bid and ask price.

But when everything seems somewhat calm, certain market institutions begin to look for points of profitable exploitation of the IPO in the active market. These institutions watch the progress of this fledgling issue from their Level II screens. Like predators, they watch the shares of Del Mar Beverages struggle during the first days of trading. Opportunity starts to present itself. These institutional predators are the other investment banking interests not involved in this particular IPO. The investment banking industry tries to put out hundreds of hollow deals, like Del Mar Beverages, per year to the individual investment sector.

Those within the stock business recognize such IPOs for what they are. The other firms see the stock price at $5 and know that it is only worth around $4 or below. They also know the full extent of buying power that the underwriting firms have in reserve, to keep the share price strong. The predator firms watch and wait for the underwriting firms' buying power to wane. Then the predators begin to sell the stock short at $5. Basically, they start selling the stock at $5, begin to drive the price down and buy it back at a lower price. As the predator firms begin the selling momentum, the traders do not have enough buy orders to match the sell orders and the stock price begins to drop. Many of the skittish individual investors begin to follow suit by selling their shares. The stock price drops even further. The rest of the market decides to stay clear of this stock, for the moment. This gives the predator firms plenty of time to cover their short position without running the stock price back up.

The predators sold the stock short at $5 and put the money into their own account. They must eventually buy back this borrowed stock. Thus, they need the individual shareholders to panic sell into the initiated selling momentum. This helps bring the share price down to about $3. At this point the predator begins to methodically buy back or cover this borrowed position. This firm made $2 per share just by sitting back, observing and waiting for the time to act. The individual investors who sold in the panic lost money in record time and those who held onto it now have a $3 stock that just carried a $5 price tag. But at least they didn't have to pay a commission for this privilege.

At the end of this first round, the stock price languishes and its trading volumes settle to a dismal level. If Del Mar Beverages has any future potential at all, quite often at this point the original underwriting firms, or even one of the predators, will begin a disciplined buying program of the stock. This buying will be in increments that won't draw attention nor push the stock price up. The position will be built up at low prices, held in reserve and saved for a future promotion.

This scenario regarding the initial public offering of Del Mar Beverages is a typical outcome of a marginal new stock deal. There have been exceptions, but the typical investor's experience with IPOs is similar to the previous results. When a company is being taken public and individual investors are able to pick up a majority of the shares in the IPO, the deal is questionable. Otherwise the investment bank would ensure the stock went to the more valued institutional clients. The relative odds and averages state the hard facts of the matter. When a client gets the opportunity for large scale participation in an IPO, the deal is going to be marginal at best and the market forces in place have them at a complete disadvantage.

The theme of this book is to convey the 20 ways you lose money on your way to the stock market. Consider these ways to be pitfalls to avoid. The investor on a mission to lose asset value will only need to participate in a few initial public offerings to experience the second, third and fourth ways you lose money.

WAY #2: *Consider yourself special when the broker is willing to do whatever is necessary to get you shares of a "hot" and oversubscribed IPO.* Be thankful your broker was so savvy that he or she knew to inflate your original indication of interest. True, you only received half of the shares you indicated an interest in, but what a coincidence it is about the size of your average position anyway. A firm that will give individual investors the opportunity to be a part of a big winner is a rare commodity, and you should take advantage. Start writing your check now.

WAY #3: *Heed your broker's advice that suggests you buy half your position as an IPO and the other half when it starts trading on the active market.* That way you already own a portion of the stock, just in case the price starts to run on the opening. The other half of the money is in reserve, just in case the price dips down ever so slightly upon the start of trading. Then you can take advantage of a lower price for a great stock. Oh, and don't forget that all this will be done for you commission-free.

WAY #4: *Don't worry about asking your broker if he or she is under a penalty bid should you decide to sell your shares within the first 30 days of trading.* Do not inquire if he or she is required by the firm to have clients buy a certain percentage of the stock as an IPO and the rest once it starts trading. If you do ask these two questions and the broker says that neither one is the case, take your broker at his or her word, because it is not like there is an ulterior motive, right? In the event that you did want to sell your shares within the first 30 days of trading, consider whatever earth-shattering reason given by your broker for not selling the stock at that particular moment to be sound. Remember, your broker is there to serve your best interest and help you to invest your money.

CHAPTER 4

Interpreting the Buy and Sell Signs in Price Spreads and Quotes

The Ways You Lose: 5, 6 and 7

The term *spread* exists in many arenas outside of the stock market. For the gambling man, the spread helps with the decision of which team to choose in the Super Bowl. A table with a fine spread is always the desired destination of the big eater. But the spread in a stock price is its least understood form, yet it represents the most predictable type of loss in the market. This spread exists within a larger mystery known as the stock quote. The investor who can grasp the spread concept and unravel the mysteries of the quote has a valuable tool to interpret the real story behind a stock's current situation.

The attainment of this valuable tool starts with a view of spreads in their primary form. It all begins with the price quote that flashes across the television screen. In its most basic structure, the quote consists of the stock's symbol and two different numbers. A typical example would be the following:

HRSE 7 7⅝

A company called Horse has a current bid of $7.00 and a current ask of $7.625. The informed individual investor can already deduce a couple of facts concerning this stock. She knows if she is selling shares of HRSE today, the price that she will get is $7.00, which is the *bid* price. The quote also tells her, if she is buying shares of HRSE, the purchase price will be $7.625, which is the *ask* price. And since she has a firm grasp of this simple quote format, another very important element becomes clear to her.

Between the bid and the ask, there is a spread of 62½ cents. This spread goes to the firm that is making the market in the stock of HRSE. Each seller into this market will receive $7 per share. The firm will take these shares and charge the next buyers $7.625 per share. The firm's profit margin off the current quote is almost 9 percent.

One of my best analogies, to explain the spread concept, is the one that relates it to a wall with two teller windows. An investor walks through the door and is confronted by a large wall, within a cavernous lobby. At the top of the wall, in capital letters, is the stock symbol HRSE. At the base of the wall are two teller windows. Above the window on the left is a sign that reads BID. Next to the word *bid,* and scribbled in chalk, is the price of $7. Above the window on the right is a sign that reads ASK. Next to the word *ask,* and also scribbled in chalk, is the price of $7.625. There is a line of people formed before each window.

The investor is a tad unsure of what to do next. She approaches the security guard with her inquiry. The guard asks her if she is buying or selling today. The investor replies that she intends to buy some shares. The guard then directs her to the ASK line. There, she waits patiently for her turn to come. When she gets to the window, she intends to purchase 1,000 shares of HRSE at the current asking price.

As she moves to the front of the line, she looks across to the BID line. Her eyes meet with those of the man in the front of that line. In his hands is a manila envelope. It is clearly marked 1,000 shares of HRSE. "Next!" is simultaneously called from both windows. He steps up to his window to sell, and she steps up to her window to buy. She states that she would like to buy 1,000 shares of HRSE at 7⅝. The teller informs her the total comes to $7,625, and starts to count the money that she placed on the counter. The teller, from the other window, comes over with the manila envelope containing the 1,000 shares of HRSE. The ASK window teller gives the investor the share certificates and hands the other teller $7,000. The remaining $625 is handed to a smiling, well-dressed man who stands in the back. He places the money in the safe and stands ready with the chalk, in case the bid or ask price needs to be adjusted.

Meanwhile, the other teller walks back to the BID window and hands the man the $7,000. He takes his money and heads out the door and down the stairs to the parking lot. There he sees the woman with her new 1,000 shares of HRSE. The two smile at one another, get into their respective cars and drive home.

The previous example might seem to be overly simplified, but it is crucial to understand the basic relationship of the buyer and the seller, and the role played by the entity in the middle. The ability to comprehend and to interpret a particular stock's spread, involves the consideration of additional factors. However, the primary connection between the three players in a stock transaction, as depicted above, must first be mastered to gain enlightenment of spread consciousness.

The entity in the middle is the firm that is making the market for a specific stock. In this case, the stock is HRSE. Being a market maker for a certain stock, the firm maintains a bid and ask arena, in which investors can buy and sell. This firm also has an obligation to provide an orderly market, within reason. This obligation can entail taking a position in the stock during a moderate sell-off. But the firm is not required to buy up an enormous amount of shares, if the price begins to crash, due to mass selling. The term market maker generally refers to over-the-counter stocks. And there could be just a few or a couple dozen market makers for a particular share issue. For exchange traded stocks, the role of market maker is generally played by a specialist.

The market making firm is comprised of many different players, but only two really matter. The brokers and the traders are the ones who provide the firm with its bottom line. Everyone else fills a position of support for the two bread-winners.

Reconsider the teller window analogy. All those people standing in line represent transaction orders that were successfully solicited by the brokers. Whether the buy line or the sell line is longer depends on which direction best serves the firm's own interest. The trader is the well-dressed man that stands behind the two window tellers. He makes sure that a little portion of each transaction goes into the firm's till, in the form of the spread. He does not need to know the stock's story like the brokers do, but he does need to anticipate market movements. If the trader senses the stock price is about to make a run up, then he will increase the firm's own position to sell into the pending strength. If the brokers do their job and bring in the buy and sell orders, the smile on the trader's face will grow as the trading volume increases.

For the buyer and seller, those on either side of the entity in the middle, the prospects for prosperity are not so certain. If the seller is taking profits just before the share price drops, or if the buyer takes a position a day before a buying frenzy, then the transactional move was well-timed. But as usual, the individual has to operate from a disadvantageous angle. It starts at the moment the stock is originally purchased. The comparison of this experience to buying a car is appropriate.

When a person finishes the process of buying a new car, the hardest part comes after it is driven off the lot. This brand-new investment on wheels suddenly attains used status when it hits the street. In a matter of seconds, the resale value drops at least 10 percent. Our buyer of HRSE had the same experience. Immediately after buying her shares at 7⅝, had she gone to the BID window to sell, she would have received only 7 for her shares. As she turned away from the ASK window, the resale value of her shares dropped almost 9 percent from the original purchase price.

We should not begrudge a reasonable spread. Market makers incur certain expenses, and they shouldn't be expected to work for free. A spread of 3½ to 5 percent is reasonable. With a spread above 8 percent, I don't know who is more out-of-line, the market makers who maintain it or the investors who buy into it. However, the spread situation can be made worse by the investors themselves. Often and without realizing it, individual investors pay both a spread and a commission when buying or selling a stock.

When an investment firm executes an investor's transaction order, it acts in either an agency or a principal capacity. The entity in the middle, as described in the HRSE example, is executing the buys and sells as a principal. Many of those people conceptually standing in front of the BID or ASK window are being represented by other investment firms that do not make a market in HRSE. This nonmarket-making firm will go to an HRSE principal firm and buy the stock for the client. The market maker will provide the stock at the higher ask price and collect the spread. The nonmarket-making firm will charge a commission to the client, for whom it is acting in an agency capacity. The client buys 1,000 shares of HRSE at the current quote of 7 by 7⅝. She buys them at the higher ask price, pays $625 in a spread of almost 9 percent and pays an estimated 4 percent commission of $305. The client just paid $7.93 a share, for a stock that has a market value of $7.

While I'm showing you the ways you lose money on your way to the stock market, here's a little advice concerning agency versus principal stock trading. If you have discovered a stock with potential, by your own research and not biased propaganda, then buy through a firm that can act as a principal for the purchase. You will only pay the spread by going to the market maker. The stock can always be transferred back to a central account of your choice. But exercise caution if a stock is being recommended to you by a firm that makes a market in its shares. True, the stock's story could have merit, but there is a good chance you are buying shares that the firm is trying to clear out of its inventory. This is a classic example of the firm making you a part of its created demand.

The Essential Basics for Understanding Spreads

Once the basics are understood, an investor can begin to read the indicators being presented by the spread. Without knowing a stock's story or situation, a quick glance at the complete quote can reveal a wealth of information. A complete quote includes a bit more information than just the stock symbol and the bid and ask prices. But first there is a relevant myth that needs to be dispelled.

On a day when a specific stock or the broader indexes take a sizable loss, a universal explanation is often heard from brokers and other market experts. It is concisely packaged in the phrase: ". . . there were more sellers than buyers."

There are always a few chuckles released in the bull pen when another broker is overheard using this line over the phone. Besides being a part of any investment professional's verbal arsenal, it is also incorrect. For a stock to be actively trading, whether it is moving up or down, there must be a buyer for every share sold. And there must be a seller for every share purchased. The price direction is caused by the selling side or the buying side overwhelming the other. If more orders are entering the market as sell orders, the amount of stock that can be sold at the current bid price will soon be depleted. The market makers will set the next bid price, at which they'll buy another certain amount of the stock from the selling public, a notch lower than the previous bid price. It works the same way if the buy orders overwhelm the amount of stock available at the current ask price.

If a stock is currently quoted at 7 by 7⅝, and the market maker has orders to sell 10,000 shares at 7 and orders to buy 10,000 shares at 7⅝, then the stock will close flat for the day. More strength on either side determines whether the stock closes up or down. Regardless of price direction, there was a buyer and a seller for every share traded. In a situation where a stock price is rising or dropping so fast that adequate buy or sell orders can't be found to match the particular direction, trading in the stock will be halted. The trading will remain stopped until the principal firms can reestablish an orderly market.

Now as an informed individual investor you can begin to build upon your primary spread comprehension. You can now read into the size of the spread. There are two more additions to the basic stock quote being used as a reference. Besides the stock symbol, the bid price and the ask price, the near complete quote includes the current trading volume and an indicator of any recently released market news. The monetary distance between the bid and the ask, combined with the two new additions to the advanced stock quote, provide an explanation behind how the stock is currently trading. You can then make a reasonable estimation as to what the share price might do next.

First consider a narrow versus a wide spread. A narrow spread can be considered reasonable. The range should be between 3.5 and 5 percent of the bid price. An example would be a stock with a bid of 7, should have an ask of approximately .25, or 3.5 percent higher. When the difference in the low and high numbers of the quote are within a reasonable percentage, it normally means the shares are trading evenly. At the current bid and ask, the number of buy and sell orders being entered are matching one another. This stock is trading in a steady market. If an investor has determined this particular stock is worth owning, the shares should be purchased during this period of even trading and narrow spread.

A wide spread can mean several different things. Usually the possibilities will not be in the individual investor's favor. Any spread above 8 percent of the bid amount should definitely be considered excessive. A market maker will often post an inflated spread to merely feel out the investing public. For the market maker, anything in-between goes to the house.

If the individual investors are willing to pay an enormous spread, the firms acting as principals for that stock are willing to charge it. The spread will remain excessive until it becomes obvious that any buying interest has backed off, well below the ask price. A market maker will post whatever spread percentage that the market will bear. Most retail clients buy a stock after considering only the broker's pitch and the ask price. Since most individual investors don't even realize the lower bid price represents their true immediate market value, they are never aware of the loss incurred during the first second of ownership. If their trade was executed on an agency basis, they can add the commission charge to their loss.

A True Tale of Extreme Spread Excess

I want to convey a real life horror story regarding this matter of spreads. As a break from tradition, I will tell the moral of the story first. Although the villains were on the inside, it was the client's own ignorance and apathy that caused all the hardship. This story demonstrates one of the ways you lose money on your way to the stock market.

The stock story pertains to a somewhat ethereal gold exploration company. The company had no earnings, no producing mines and no real assets. The total shares outstanding were just under a million. With no redeeming qualities or inspiring reasons to buy the stock, the trading volume for Golden Rail was usually between zero and 1,000 shares a day. Even more pathetic was that the bid price was at 25 cents. And there was no fundamentally sound reason for the shares to go up in value any time soon. This sham publicly traded equity instrument would prove to be quite lucrative for a couple of slick guys with a plan.

A broker in La Jolla, California had acquired just over 400,000 shares of Golden Rail. He had amassed over half the outstanding shares by means other than buying off the market. The broker knew the company had all the appeal of a tax audit, and the share price was going nowhere fast. He would have to become extremely creative if any money was to be made from this worthless stock. This broker did not have access to a powerful propaganda machine, nor did he have a giant client base. So an expensive, rapid-fire promotional campaign was not an option. The key to success, for this shepherd of the shady shares, was to covertly charge the mother of all spreads.

The Golden Rail company would not interfere with the broker's efforts, because it had been worn down to a part-time operation and didn't even bother to maintain an investor relations phone line anymore. Since the market maker was not part of the same broker dealer firm as the La Jolla broker, both a spread and a commission could be charged. But more importantly, this broker with the nearly half million share block was aligned with the stock's only market maker. The situation was ripe for making a quick buck.

The broker deposited all the shares with the market maker. The two agreed to set the quote at .25 by $2.50. They planned to take a spread of almost 1,000 percent. It would be an excellent pay-off, especially compared to what the broker and the market maker considered to be minimal risk.

There was no concern of any regulatory agency flagging down the ridiculous spread percentage, because absolutely no one paid attention to the happenings of Golden Rail stock. Any eventual back-lash of the enraged clients would not hamper the execution of the plan. The broker's client book consisted of small accounts and portfolios of once decent monetary stature that had been churned down to near oblivion. With his book smoldering and on the brink of total combustion, the broker figured on one last jab before he moved his act to a new town. Within 90 days, he would pawn off the block of shares, and he would just stall the shareholders until the entire amount was unloaded.

The broker and the market maker decided not to charge a commission on top of their spread, because at a nearly 1,000 percent profit margin, it was best to put as much funds into the stock as possible. For every $2,000 of client assets put into the Golden Rail stock, 800 shares would be unloaded and the two collaborators would net $1,800 dollars in the spread. The broker just called down his client list and promised that this stock play would make everything right again. The buy orders were entered and the market maker maintained the spread in the original position. Four hundred thousand shares were passed to the noninstitutional clients for a profit of $900,000. By the time any of the shareholders discovered the true market value of their shares, both broker and market maker were long gone to new pastures.

Although it is easy to determine who the bad guys were in this story, the clients were partially to blame. The only reason that the evil duo thought they could get away with it was that they both knew, all too well, that typical individual investors don't consider the spread. And if they do, they rarely check what they are quoted against a second market source, before entering a buy order. This example of the 1,000 percent spread is extreme and could only be done under desperate or temporary conditions. The point is that excessive spreads will be left in place, as long as investors are willing to pay them.

Reading the Real Story Behind the Spread

Besides the motives of a greedy market maker, the presence of a wide spread can be the result of sudden buying or selling pressure being applied to the stock. Drastic moves in the share price will lead to excessive differences between the bid and ask prices. Two more revealing additions to our basic quote will help you understand the meaning behind a wide spread. The current quote for HRSE is 5 by 5¾ and is down by $2. So far into the day's trading, you will normally see the current trading volume to be well above its average. The quote will include an asterisk that indicates related news has just been released. This more complete quote would appear in the following format:

HRSE * 5 5¾ -2 v2,000,000 (Often the last three zeros are omitted.)

This quote scenario, with its volume increase, recent news release and excessive spread, would be the same if the drastic share price move was upward. Regardless of the direction of price movement, a period of excessive spread is not the proper time to buy the stock.

For the next example, the stock in question is making a major move up in price. A half an hour into the market day, the share price has already made a sizable jump. The quote flashes across the bottom of the financial news screen:

HRSE * 8½ 9⅜ +1½ v1,300,000

The commentator is conveying the story related to the current propulsion of HRSE's share price. The +1½ indicates the share price is currently up $1.50 from the opening quote. The Horse company released news that one of its wonder products received FDA approval. The news release was quickly followed with increased earning estimates by two national investment firms. The commentator closes the story by stating that buyers have been flocking to the stock since the market opened, 30 minutes earlier. The individual investor, watching from home, is left in an anxious state. His mind starts to race as he searches for his brokerage firm's number, and his dialing finger begins to itch.

If this individual investor makes the call and buys into the current frenzy, the odds are high that it will turn out to be a mistake. For he is basing his investment decision on a created sense of urgency. The news story has effectively appealed to his emotion of greed, but the story failed to convey a few crucial aspects. The most obvious missing piece is any emphasis on the current spread. (Perhaps the omission is because the television producer feels that those individuals who do not understand the concept of spread should not be putting their funds in the stock market.) The current spread is just over 10 percent and with a standard commission, the motivated investor jumps in and starts approximately 15 percent in the hole.

The market makers for HRSE can see the multitudes coming before the stampede begins. These principal firms are aware that the news and the media coverage, combined with major analysts putting buy ratings on HRSE, will bring the herd running with their wallets and purses open.

The anticipation caused the stock to open a bit higher. In the first few seconds of the trading session, the market makers filled the buy orders for their preferred institutional clients. This sudden blast of massive buying power overwhelmed the amount of stock that was up for sale around the opening quote. Within a few moments the share price was up close to a point and a half ($1.50), and the spread was increased above 10 percent.

By the time the individual investor entered his buy order, there were at least two strikes against him. The 15 percent excessive spread and commission deficit were accompanied by a substantially higher share price that already reflected the bulk of the good news. The investor bought with the hope that the current price run would continue to progress. Although the reality of that hope was anyone's guess, there was another omission in the financial news dialogue that could have helped the investor make a prudent decision.

The other missing reference was any mention of HRSE's current trading volume. The stock had a current trading volume of 1,300,000 shares at the time of the news story. The stock, which normally had traded an average of 50,000 shares a day for the past quarter, was now trading at a volume 26 times its recent norm. Remember the old rule: If your stock price is to go up, more people must buy the stock after you than before you.

HRSE was trading well beyond its normal volume. If the volume could stay steady or increase, after the purchase, the investor could probably have done okay. If the inflated trading volume began to fall back towards the norm or the selling began to overwhelm the buying power, the share price would not have been able to remain at its lofty heights. The odds are good that the investor bought the stock at the short term price zenith. Unless even more buyers could be found, the new shareholder will have paid a premium for what would soon be a lower-priced stock.

An addition can be made to complete the stock quote, available to individual investors. This addition was not included in the condensed quote that flashed across the screen during the delivery of the related news story. The quote now reads:

HRSE * 8½ 9⅜ +1 1½ v1,300,000 8000 X 75,000

The bid and ask share size of the current quote would be added after the current trading volume figure. The current bid size of 8,000 shares means that the market could absorb that amount of shares being sold at 8½ without the bid price moving down. The current ask size of 75,000 shares indicates that more than that amount of stock has to be bought from the market at 9⅜, before the share price can move up.

If this part of the quote had been included and considered, the investor might have ascertained it would take much more power to push HRSE up to the next level, compared with the slight selling pressure that could cause the share price slip. When the current bulge of trading volume is considered, it is more probable that the buying frenzy and trading activity will taper off, and the share price will start to come down.

The Signs of the Acceptable Spread

The theme of the previous examples, stresses the importance of spread consciousness and consideration of the complete quote when making a transactional decision. Regardless of the source, an investor should not accept or act upon a quote unless it contains all the components. The complete quote for HRSE is full of tips that are all advising the reader not to buy the stock during the current price run. Extremes are present throughout the quote of this stock, currently on a run up. Until moderation has returned to the components of the quote, it would not be a sound decision to buy shares.

The advice is the same when considering the purchase of a stock that is dropping in price. A stock should not be purchased when extremes exist in its quote components. Consider a previous example used for

HRSE during a down-slide. The bid and ask size have been added for completeness:

HRSE * 5 5¾ -2 v2,000,000 40,000 X 8,000

Until moderation returns to the various aspects of the quote, the share price has probably not reached its short-term bottom. There is no need to buy a stock while it is still on its way down.

The informed individual investor should know the spread before considering the purchase of any stock. The review and comprehension of the complete quote should be a primary part of the decision-making process. These simple concepts will be the investor's guide to what not, and when not to buy. Investors can increase their chances for success by properly timing the decision to purchase shares. But even an investor who understands the spread and has a complete quote to consider can still be at a disadvantage to the technology of the market institutions. The specific piece of technology is known as the Level II screen. The real advantage, for those who have access to its images, is not always significant, but the function of the Level II screen should be understood.

The Distinct Advantage of Technology

An investment firm uses a Level II screen to view the depth of buying and selling interest around a stock's current quote. This vantage point goes well beyond the bid and ask size. A reading of 8,000 X 30,000 reveals the first level of stock available at the bid of 7 and the ask of 7⅝. The individual investor cannot see how many other orders are stacked up to sell into the market at 7⅛ and up, and in what size blocks. Also, she cannot see how many are lined up to buy the stock at 7½ and below, and in what share amounts.

With a current quote of 7 by 7⅝ with 8,000 X 30,000 shares on either side, those investors who accept this stock's current sell and buy prices can do either transaction within the posted bid and ask sizes. But without access to the Level II screen, the individual investor cannot see what lies beyond the stock's current first level of liquidation and purchase availability. Even if an individual investor properly considers the complete quote, she cannot determine whether there is a massive amount of selling or buying intentions laying in wait, just beyond the stock's current market. However, this broader picture of the stock's current circumstances can be viewed by the investment firms. And they use this privileged information to their distinct advantage.

Let's first assume the current bid and ask sizes are even. There are 15,000 shares that can be sold into the market for 7, and there are 15,000 shares that can be purchased from the market at 7⅝. Without considering the size of the spread, any recent news releases or unusual trading volumes, an individual investor might still be well timed in buying into such an even market. But access to a Level II screen would provide a much clearer short-term view, related to the timing of the purchase decision.

With 15,000 shares on either side of the current market for HRSE, the individual investor can determine what amount of buying power must be injected to push up the share price. If an order to buy 20,000 shares was entered, the market maker would normally adjust the quote to 7⅛ by 7¾, with new bid and ask sizes. What the investor cannot see are the market forces that could be waiting to pounce on the share price. If there is a large amount of orders stacked up to sell HRSE stock once the bid reaches 7⅛, then selling pressure is going to hit the stock immediately.

If the sell orders in waiting add up to 75,000 shares at 7⅛, then that amount will have to be absorbed into the market before the share price can rise above this mark. Every time the bid and ask moves up to 7⅛ by 7¾, the current amount available to be sold at 7⅛ will reduce the 75,000 shares stacked up and waiting to be sold. This block of selling pressure will serve as a temporary restraining force on the share price. It is not the time to buy if there are massive amounts of sell orders waiting just above your purchase price. This is where a Level II screen becomes valuable.

There are limitations on the effectiveness of spreads and quotes, in the hands of those with bad motives, coupled with the naiveté of individual investors. Excessive spreads will be maintained as long as there are people willing to pay them. Incomplete quotes will be given to and considered by individual investors as long as they continue not to ask for all the vital numbers and don't learn to read the complete stock quote. Although it will be tough for individual investors to ever gain access to a Level II screen, as a savvy investor, you need to realize that those who pass out the recommendations are often looking at this short-term market crystal ball.

Each new addition to your stock market understanding strengthens your skill and enhances your success as an investor. Your new conceptual grasp of spreads and quotes enables you to recognize the following ways you lose money on your way to the stock market.

WAY #5: *Don't spend the time or effort to call another market source and double-check the bid and ask that you were just quoted.* In the few minutes required to ensure you're not paying an excessive spread, you could miss a major run-up in share price. Well, it could happen.

WAY #6: *In the name of convenience, after deciding which stock to buy, pick any firm to buy it for you.* Your firm will act in an agency capacity and buy from another firm that is a principal market maker in the stock. Although you will pay the agency's commission and the principal's spread, you'll make two firms very happy, instead of just one.

WAY #7: *Consider only the ask price when buying a stock and only the bid when selling.* Considering the complete quote is a time-consuming inquiry and a lengthy learning process. All the different informative aspects of a complete stock quote would provide too many points of insight when trying to time an investment decision. It's much easier to practice the popular technique of entering the order and hoping for the best.

CHAPTER 5

Examination of Ulterior Motives Behind Specific Stock Recommendations

The Ways You Lose: 8, 9 and 10

More dangerous than yelling "Blue light special, aisle 5!" in a crowded K-mart is the phrase, "Let me tell you which stock you should be buying now." There are only two pure forms of financial market investment: stocks and bonds. An interest yield objective dictates the purchase of bonds. Of course a stable utility company with a decent dividend can also do the trick. For capital gain or growth of principal objectives, the appropriate vehicle is a straight stock play. And every professional member of the investment population has a specific recommendation to offer.

The Ultimate Necessity of Stock Investing

It eventually happens to even the most loyal mutual fund investors. They realize their aspirations for substantial capital gains will not be accomplished by this packaged, holding pattern of an investment product. Most mutual fund companies create an arena in which individual investors will feel an inexplicable sense of comfort and will be motivated to contribute their funds in relatively generous allotments. Unfortunately, these mutual fund investors usually make their donations without a particular objective or strategy in mind. Somewhere in their past, these investors embraced the idea of placing their money in these environments of fiscal sedation. We will be covering the losing ways of mutual fund investing in Chapter 10.

For now, let's say, as a dissatisfied mutual fund investor you are ready to leave your comfortable womb in search of capital gain potential. You join the group of individuals already toiling in the straight stock arena. The majority of this group spend their investment lives repeating the same mistakes, most of which originate from their premarket decisions. As a newly converted mutual fund investor, you are likely to adopt the same practices.

The barrage of specific stock recommendations will come like an avalanche of late night infomercials. The prudent individual should realize the majority of these recommendations are biased and self-serving. Therefore, the first thoughts that come to your mind should not be the consideration of a stock purchase. As an investor, your initial reaction should be the emergence of two questions within your decision criteria.

You should first ask yourself why you are so fortunate to be the recipient of this fine stock recommendation? It could be merely a coincidence. You could be just lucky to be able to answer the phone when the call of opportunity chooses to give you a ring. It is possible your portfolio is of the stature that demands extra-special stock tips from your investment firm. Perhaps your account value is in the high six-digit or even seven-digit neighborhood. However, it is rare that an individual investor would possess a portfolio of this size. It is important to answer the question of why. To believe that decent stock recommendations are passed out like complimentary cocktails, a person would actually have to believe that something of true value can be obtained for free.

The popular response to the question of why is often: " Because the investment professional who presented the recommendation wants my portfolio to do well, so he'll keep my investment business."

The previous statement incorrectly assumes the firm for which this investment professional works makes the bulk of its profits from the commissions generated in the individual client's account. It is the investment banking business, such as underwriting new and secondary issues, making markets in stocks, and fees from promotional endeavors that provides a firm with the major portion of its earnings. The firm knows if its current client book were to blow up there are thousands more individual investors waiting to be brought on board.

The individual client is not of significant value. Only the market muscle of an amassed client base is of importance.

The second question you should ask yourself is difficult to answer: What are the ulterior motives of the entity presenting the tip? If investors embrace the idea that no sound market advice comes for free or by chance, and that their own individual success isn't the first priority of their investment firm, then the recommendation must first benefit its creator. Even if a stock tip is fundamentally sound, the time frame in which it is presented can work against those individuals who act upon it. It is not easy to make investment decisions in the wake of all the possible ulterior motives. This difficulty is magnified by the wide variety of sources that spew forth specific stock advice.

The Angle of the Brokerage Source

The most obvious and recognizable source is the investment brokerage firm. Regardless of its size, every brokerage house can be expected to provide its own list of printed and verbal stock recommendations, with its own supporting research. These packages of advice are thrust upon all clients and prospects. The firm's objective is to entice the client base to buy a particular stock, within a concentrated period of time. It is in the brokerage house's best interest that a certain stock moves in price at the right moment. If a few clients happen to make money, that's fine but not necessary. What is necessary is that the individual investors are driven, like a herd, into the desired stock. The benefit to the firm is not the measly 5 percent transaction commissions. Such spoils as spreads, investment banking fees and unloading shares from its own inventory provide the real profit margin.

As an individual investor, you should handle a specific stock recommendation from a brokerage firm with a healthy dose of cynicism. You should realize many firms view you as the expendable link in their market endeavors. And there are more naive clients available where you came from. Unless you can find a reason why your account warrants special treatment, you should suspect the presence of another motive behind the recommendation, other than for your own monetary benefit.

The Sometimes Destructive Influence of the Financial Media

The second source of specific stock recommendations is less obvious but can be more persuasive than the first. The vehicles of financial news and market information are constantly pumping out influential observations and advice.

Whether the news format is the televised nightly market report or the cover of a national financial news magazine, its powerful message reaches millions of people. A positive review of a particular stock or market sector will send the related share prices on an upward run. There is no mystery as to why the featured stock's trading volume and share price make the sudden jump. Individual investors, receiving these mass media delivered stock recommendations, will form a herd and stampede into the featured positions. Unfortunately for such investors, their buying frenzy has been anticipated by the people on the other side of the phone.

Before joining a news driven buying frenzy, the individual investor should consider a point of market reality: The good news is often already reflected in the stock price. Before the next trading day, the opening quotes are pushed up and the spreads are widened in preparation for the pending buying strength. The institutions that have the recently newsworthy stocks in their inventories try to determine the most efficient share increments in which to feed the coming demand. Never forget that the law of gravity is present in the stock market, like anywhere else.

Imagine a baseball being thrown, in a high arc, across a field. Much more effort is exerted to send the ball upward than is required for it to come down the other side. This analogy also applies to share price movement. As the public is driven to buy a certain stock, in a concentrated period of time, someone has to provide the shares that are to be frantically purchased. This supply to the demand comes mainly from institutional inventories. On the way up, these institutions try not to overwhelm the market with available shares, in order to get the most mileage in price gain. During the run-up, each new bid and ask quote will be pushed higher by the continued buying demand.

Eventually, the buying frenzy begins to taper off. The size of the sell and buy sides of the current quote approach an even balance. The share price reaches the zenith of its current upward run. Those who still hold the stock feed the last remnants of buying interest. Soon the size of selling interest begins to surpass the buying side, and the price starts to drop with the decreasing trading volume.

A portion of the original buying herd will panic in the face of this turn of events. Individual sell orders will begin to accumulate and drive the stock down further. The institutions that originally held this stock in their inventories will pull out all but a token amount of buying interest, during this drop. When the trading volume, news coverage, and the selling and buying interest return to the prehype norms, these institutions will often refill their inventories and wait for the next buying frenzy.

The unfortunate individual investor should have wondered why these member institutions were so eager to give up a stock that recently received such rave reviews by the news media. It is because the entities that dwell within the market jungle do not become emotionally involved with their share positions. To those on the inside, a stock is merely a few capital letters with some fluctuating numbers blinking after them. Regardless of the cause of the buying demand, if the public wants what an institution holds in its inventory, the request will not be denied. For a stock is a completely intangible investment, and when a crowd is driven to buy from your own ethereal stash, it is a good day— especially if the asking price is moving up.

The Publicly Traded Company Banging Its Own Drum

The publicly traded companies are the third source of specific stock recommendations. Most public companies maintain a designated phone line by which investor relations are maintained. A shareholder or an interested individual can call the company to ask questions or request information. Within the proper spectrum of inquiry, the investor relations line can provide sound answers. Annual reports, dividend payment dates, times of upcoming shareholder meetings and locations of current operations are the types of data that can be objectively provided by the company. The individual who attempts to find buy signals from the dialogue with investor relations personnel is moving dangerously close to financial self sabotage.

In most circumstances, it is in the company's best interest to attract steady buying strength to its shares. Stock option and incentive plans always seem more appealing when share prices are moving up. From the switchboard operator to the CEO, the conveyed outlook for the company is going to be positive and upbeat. The bias of this recommendation source should be obvious, yet thousands of retail investors make their market purchases according to what they hear on an investor relations line. It is very rare for a company to, even remotely, suggest that now is not the time to buy its stock.

The Most Dangerous Source Can Be Found Among Your Peers

The remaining sources of specific stock recommendations are entities that do not exist within the market jungle. These external civilian sources hover around the individual investor's daily life and spew falsehoods and market misinterpretations. These amateur ministers of misinformation can be more damaging to a portfolio's net asset value than the smoothest professional from the other side of the phone.

The most influential of these external sources is the paranoid office associate who already owns a particular stock. He keeps his paranoia pent up inside him, but he is definitely nervous about the prospects of his new market position. In the same theme of misery loves company, he decides he would feel better if those around him shared in his market risk.

I am always amazed at the amount of merit that individual investors place in the market words of their outside brethren. The girl in the exercise class or the person one is dating seems to have valuable insight, merely because they were previously convinced to buy the stock. True, there are numerous, questionable sources of specific stock recommendations from inside the market. These must be sifted through, but bad advice becomes much worse when it comes to you secondhand.

The Proper Care and Handling of the Various Sources

A level investment playing field is attainable for the individual investor, but this requires the individual to use a protective filter when considering the barrage of specific stock recommendations. Nothing can be done to circumvent the unavoidable types of market risk, such as natural disasters, sudden interest rate jumps or national scandals, that can spur a sell off and bring individual share prices down. But a general criterion can be implemented by the layperson to avoid committing the obvious mistakes.

To act upon any specific stock recommendation without consulting your personal filter is an excellent way to perpetuate a tradition of losing investment endeavors. Whether the recommendation source is from inside or outside the market jungle, all suggestions should face the scrutiny of a relatively simple mental review gauntlet. Taking a filtered approach to a specific stock recommendation begins with a cooling-off period.

The feeling that a tremendous opportunity could evaporate due to hesitation is among the most fatal sensations for an individual investor. Quick decisions, involving six- and seven-digit transactions, are the concern of institutional traders and money managers. The individual investor does not work with large enough piles of money to justify the risk of snap decisions just to make a few percentage points. You as an individual investor can afford the luxury of calm consideration and can keep funds in cash while looking for the next opportunity. Let the suckers make poor investment and fall prey to their institutional counterparts.

The wise and learned investors hesitate the moment they hear the specific stock recommendation. They absorb the pitch and refuse to make a snap decision. This is done to prevent the emotions of greed or fear from inducing a potentially disastrous transaction order. It is a constant source of aggravation for stock brokers when someone actually wants to think about a recommended stock purchase—especially if it is near the end of the production month.

Accept the fact that there will always be another opportunity available in the stock market. Recognize that even if a market source did have the very last stock opportunity, that source wouldn't be calling you with it. And if brokers did run out of unique opportunities, someone just like me would simply create a new one. As an individual investor, realize your place in the timely market information food chain. By the time the late-breaking news reaches you, everyone on the inside is waiting to sell you their shares. If an individual buys a stock because of a sense of urgency, he or she is almost always making a mistake. The investor must rebuff the herd mentality and invest according to his or her own sound criteria, and not ones that have been thrust upon him or her.

Whether the cooling-off period lasts three days or three weeks, there will be ample time to conduct a few simple reality checks. If the source of the specific stock recommendation scoffs at the wisdom of taking time to consider the merits of the transactional suggestion, that should be the first red flag of avoidance. The first of the reality checks involves close scrutiny of the stock's complete and current price quote. Consider all the aspects of the aforementioned spreads and quotes. The prospective investor should be able to answer the following questions: Is the spread between the bid and the ask excessive? Is there a recent news release already reflected in the share price? Are the share sizes on either side of the current quote out of balance? Has there already been substantial movement in the stock recently? Is the stock currently trading at much higher than normal volumes? If the answer to the majority of these questions is yes, that should be the second red flag to avoid the stock.

Compare the answers to the previous questions with the stock's price and volume chart for the last six months. These can be found with online computer services or in the library's business reference section. This chart should be augmented with a list of the last six months of news releases pertaining to the stock. Be sure to note any mentions of which firms have been promoting it. This chart will show the share price line and the corresponding trading volume for that particular day. A common theme of these graphic relative displays is that, during periods of sharp upturns in price, there is a direct correlation with drastic increases in trading volume. The time frame represented, before the price and volume increases, can hold the most valuable information for the individual investor.

The first observation should be of how the stock traded during flat market periods. If the share price stayed flat at $5, for several weeks, and had stable volumes of 20,000 shares per day, then that can serve as a reference point: This stock can maintain a share price of $5 with normal daily trading volumes of 20,000 shares. Compare the characteristics of the stable periods with those of the most recent time frame, when this stock was being recommended to you. Most likely the volumes will be at least three times the norm, and the share price will be spiking up. This third red flag should be bigger than the others and be waving vigorously. Can you hear the pounding hooves of the thundering stampede?

It is very important to reexamine the periods of stability, before this stock was brought to your attention. Look closely at the consecutive days with flat prices and steady trading volumes. There is a good chance someone figured out the exact amount of stock that could be purchased each day without running the share price up. It's also a good bet there were not many news releases or promotions during this period. There is an even better chance the savvy market player amassed a sizable position over this quiet lull. It is quite probable that whoever accomplished this task of covert stock accumulation is from the same entity telling you to buy the shares now. It is a classic example of establishing a supply and then creating a demand to sell into for a profit.

Beyond the close scrutiny of the current quote and of the price/volume chart, there are other recommendation filtration steps to take. Dissect the stock pitch, whether it is in verbal, printed or televised format. Pinpoint the objectives touted in the recommendation. A compelling reason should be given to justify buying shares of the featured company. This reason is usually packaged with the prediction of a certain event to spur a run up in the stock price. Keep in mind that if your stock is to go up in the near term, more people must want to buy it after you than before you. Thus the stated objective must be separated from the hype and checked for accuracy.

Phrases such as "expanding globally" and "explosive estimated earnings growth" will do absolutely nothing to increase your stock's value. Although the recommendation source is excited and enthusiastic about this unique, dynamic, revolutionary and exclusive market opportunity, there is still a good chance your purchase of the stock will qualify you for the sucker of the month club. Disregard all the pitch components that sound even remotely cheesy. Locate the part that encapsulates the why and the where of this stock's near future. Something must occur to attract a wave of buying interest in these shares. If a plausible reason why and a resultant destination for the stock price is not apparent in the pitch, the recommendation should be dropped from the investment consideration list. When you first hear the pitch, hang up the phone, turn off the television, put down the newspaper or close the lunchroom door. A few reality checks can be made to determine if someone is trying to insult your intelligence. Consider the following example:

The featured company is about to buy out a competitor, thus doubling the size of its current operations. The share price should go well above $10.

The vital portion has been isolated. Refer back to the stock's price and volume chart for the previous six months. Consult the list of any pertinent news releases for this time frame. The current buy price is $7 per share. The rest of the quote indicates the current trading volume is just over 750,000 shares. The chart reveals the average price, over the last stable 120-day period, was $5 per share. The trading volume, during this steady time, averaged 50,000 each day. The chart also shows that, within the last six trading days, the stock has moved up two dollars and the daily volume began to climb steadily. In the last two days the share price has moved to $7, and the daily volume has been peaking at one million shares traded. This stock was just recommended to you. Now you must decide if this is the prudent time to buy some shares.

Something has attracted a wave of buying interest to this stock. You check the list of recent news releases related to the company. There is no definite mention or prediction of the acquisition. Either it has already been anticipated by the market and reflected in the stock price, or the pitched possibility has already enticed a sufficient number of people to buy before you and made the price move. Whatever the case, this presents a probable paradox to those individuals contemplating a share purchase at this point. If the acquisition occurs, then the potential increase in share price has already happened during the anticipation driven buying strength. If the acquisition does not occur or proves to be falsely predicted, then the disappointment and recent buyers' remorse will induce a sell off and resultant share price drop.

The prudent individual investor will also check the reality of the predicted share price target. A stock that was recently trading steady at $5 is projected to move above $10. It takes quite a bit of impulse to push a share price to double. Especially if the size of the public share float or shares outstanding is considered. The side information on the chart lists the company's outstanding share float at 30 million shares. That means before the share price started its run, the company's market capitalization was $150 million. If the stock were to reach the $10 projection, then the market capitalization would be $300 million. This type of substantial increase would require an incredibly powerful and sustained buying frenzy. If you are considering buying at $7 per share, before the sizable trading volume increase, your investment success is too dependent on the likelihood of the necessary and continued buying strength.

The Proper Frame of Mind

The last step to the recommendation filtration process is conducted completely within the potential investor's mind. The old cliché that endorses the use of common sense also applies to stock market investing. Does the above investment endeavor seem sensible to you? One can never be certain of any market outcome. A high degree of probability is the highest level of confidence that can be attained beforehand. It is very difficult to determine if a recommendation source is credible. The mere fact that the pitch comes from an entity with a broker dealer license in no way makes it any more valid than if it came from the guy mowing your lawn. At least you can reasonably assume the guy mowing your lawn isn't trying to push the stock on you, out of his own inventory.

After the complete quotes have been reviewed, the charts and news releases have been checked, the objectives have been determined and the ulterior motives have been considered, ask yourself if the stock still has a reasonable chance of success. If you answer yes, and the proposed move passes the same common sense criteria you use with other life decisions, then buy the stock. At the very least you avoided the preventable mistakes related to stock investing. You haven't been hastily driven by your own emotions of greed or fear. You haven't fallen victim to someone else's created sense of urgency or ulterior motive. You've been able to gauge your entry position in relation to the overall progress of the stock's current move. Thus, you have a reasonable chance of not being part of the last group of investors left holding the bag.

Individual investors are constantly held at a distinct disadvantage by the system. However, this disadvantage is definitely surmountable. Be of sound and cynical mind when approaching the stock market. Consider the ulterior motive of any source, ostensibly altruistic enough to grant you an exclusive stock recommendation. Everyone has an angle and they are all competing with you for profits in the market. Realize any intelligent being is capable of forming a successful investment philosophy and strategy. Most individual investors lose in the stock market due to their own ignorance and apathy. The majority of these losses are avoidable and occur while the funds are on the way to the market. There is no real safety in numbers if you are part of the herd thundering into a stock position. If you purchase the same stock as everyone else in your office, and they all received the recommendation from the same firm or other source of promotional materials, you may find yourself in a very precarious position.

These passages are dedicated to exposing the fine art of losing money. This art form has been perfected by the throngs of individual investors who have donated their funds to many a market endeavor over the years. As a tribute to those esteemed and valiant guardians of the lost market cause, I present the specific stock recommendation's eighth, ninth and tenth ways you lose money on your way to the stock market.

WAY #8: *Be sure to have plenty of company when buying into a stock position.* An enormous amount of people, all buying a particular stock within a short period of time, can't be all wrong. Just think of the fools who are parting with their precious shares and selling into your buying frenzy.

WAY#9: *By whatever means and from whatever source the recommendation is presented, seize the moment.* In the short time it takes to check the volume, news and promotion relativity, a great opportunity could have passed you by. The common sense criteria that you implement with other decisions in life don't necessarily apply to your investment endeavors.

WAY #10: *Take your pick, for portfolio guidance, from the great sources of investment advice available.* Friends, neighbors or office associates can be excellent purveyors of sound market strategy. If your investment firm, your medium of information, and the particular company's investor relations personnel are all in agreement, consider that to be the ultimate buy signal.

CHAPTER 6

How Block Trades Work Against the Individual Investor

The Ways You Lose: 11

Block Trading as an Institutional Tool

At some point, the retail investor will be introduced to the concept of block trades. This introduction normally manifests itself in an offer to participate in such a trade. The broker usually includes a considerable dose of hype and urgency with the presentation, due to the time-sensitive nature of the endeavor.

The block trade is an important tool used by the institutions that derive their livelihood from the stock market. When a securities firm targets a certain stock for bulk acquisition, there are inherent obstacles to overcome. Consider the example of a publicly traded mining company named KingSol. The securities firm has determined that six months from now it would be advantageous to have a big position of the stock in its inventory.

KingSol is currently trading at 2½ by 2¾. The price has been steady and its average trading volume has been at 20,000 shares a day. Thus, approximately $50,000 worth of this stock changes hands during each recent trading session. KingSol Mining has 15 million shares outstanding. The firm wants to acquire 5 percent of the company's public float, about 750,000 shares.

The current bid and ask price of any stock is merely a temporary reflection of its relative supply versus demand. The stock's average trading volume gauges the investing public's present interest. If the firm approached the current market for KingSol Mining with 750,000 shares worth of buying demand, the trading balance would be quickly overwhelmed. The traders would scramble to locate stock on the sell side to satisfy the appetite of the massive buy order. The buying momentum would rapidly multiply as the herd of investors watched the stock begin to move. The share price would skyrocket.

Eventually the firm would have their shares, but there would be a wide range of fill prices for the entire buy order. The colossal buy order would instantly absorb the stock available for buying on the ask side at 2¾, then at 3, then at 3½ and so on. The traders would have to let the market run to fill the demand. This buy order, that started to be filled at 2¾, would go as high as 12½ to complete. Of course, this would never have happened. A securities firm would never enter a buy order this way, especially if it was their own money at risk.

If a securities firm really wanted to acquire a large position in a certain stock, the process would all start with the senior partners of the firm. One of the senior partners would make a few calls from a very exclusive phone list. The phone numbers belong to the inside players of the stock market.

KingSol Mining, and those who represent the major shareholders of the company, would then receive a phone call from the interested firm. The senior partner would keep his inquiry subtle and discreet. He would mention that there was a certain party with a remote interest in acquiring a nice little piece of KingSol Mining stock, if it could be done at a reasonable price. Unless there is a compelling reason that the shares should be held, institutional sellers can usually be found. The big players do not become emotionally involved with their stock positions. A fraction of a point up, on a bulk position, means hefty net profits. They'll take the money off the table and call it a good week.

The block of 750,000 shares of KingSol could come from a single institution. The buyer and the seller coordinate the time and price. The traders representing both sides of the transaction are given their instructions. At a specific time, the trader on the selling side will put the enormous block of KingSol into the market, usually just above the bid price. One second after, the trader from the buying side will hit that bid and pick up the entire amount of shares. The transaction is complete in a matter of seconds. The current trading volume total is suddenly increased by 750,000 shares, and everybody knows a huge block of stock was just crossed.

This is the procedure for a firm that wants to buy a stock for its own inventory. Often this type of stock will be the subject of a future promotion. At the very least, the firm will play the role of supplier, if the stock should start to run up on externally driven demand. This type of block trading method is the same if the firm wants to quickly, and quietly, sell a large stock position from its own inventory.

How the Block Trade Trap Is Set

The methods and motives for block trading become very different when the individual investors are involved. For an investment firm to pursue the fruits of advanced block trading, it is absolutely crucial that it has an expansive investor account book at its disposal. In this new arena, the time constraints are much tighter. Stock positions must move, between the institution and the individual accounts, within a single trading day. This ensures the institution's market risk is kept to a minimum.

The rewards to the institution come in various overt and covert forms. Before the end of the market day, the individual accounts have assumed the risk of holding the stocks involved. The investment firm has a few profitable motives to engage in block trading with their individual accounts. I will present these motives in the next few pages. But first, regardless of the particular plan of the day, it is always packaged to the client in the same fashion.

The concept, touted to the client, is heavily laden with emotional stimulants. Greed is the preferred emotion, and fear is always there for a backup. The naive stock investor does all the groundwork to set himself up for the kill. He reminds his broker to give him a call when something looks "hot" or at least "really good." The client's name is put with the others on the speed list. Within a couple weeks, a branch manager or a senior partner informs the staff of a special project. The raw details are digested. The brokers manipulate the information into an appealing format to be shoved through the phone.

This new project does not involve the firm's own investment account. The firm will be acting in a pure broker capacity. The relative time constraints justify the manufactured sense of urgency. The trading day lasts for only six hours, or six and a half, if you are on the Vancouver exchange. That is not a lot of time to get this message of hope to the people. The senior partner yells "charge!" and the story-tellers scramble back to the bull pen.

Out to the masses goes the packaged promise of possibility. Such good fortune can go to those lucky enough to answer their phone. A broker might start with something like this: "Mr. Nathon, I remembered what you said about getting back to you when a special situation presents itself. Well it took a couple of weeks, but I've finally seen something extraordinary. Our senior analyst discovered it yesterday, just after the end of trading. The company's name is Pompey Mining. They have been conducting large scale exploratory drilling in Nevada's Carlin Trend area. The drill results are due to be published at anytime. All our previous intelligence suggested that the news will be outstanding, but the strongest indicator quietly occurred yesterday afternoon. Our trader began to see large blocks of Pompey Mining stock being accumulated by certain market players. A closer look at these players revealed that they represent interests extensively involved in events surrounding the Carlin Trend. Our analyst sees this as confirmation of our original research. The discreet buying of the stock, by those close to the source, speaks very highly of the drill results and the moment of those results being released is upon us. Of course, our firm and our clients want to be in position before the news is announced and then reflected in the share price."

Now the why of the matter has been established. This typical, aggressive stock investor starts to feel the excitement. He thinks he's finally in on a major market development before it happens. If this client is to be sold on the proposal, it will be because the firm has complete confidence in the position. This is best demonstrated to the client by conveying the firm's endorsement through a commitment of its own capital.

"When the market opened this morning, our trader took down a large block of Pompey Mining stock for our firm's account. We are committed financially and strategically to this position. We're confident that this move is going to pay off extremely well. Now the senior partners have reserved a portion of this block for the clients who want to participate. I don't have a tremendous amount of the stock available per account, but I can probably get 2,000 shares for you (the amount of capital in his average stock position). But if you don't want it, that's okay; I'll let some other clients in on the deal. I wanted to call you first since I promised to let you in on the next opportunity."

No self-respecting stock jockey, with aggressive return aspirations, could pass up a pitch like this. He sees this as his chance to execute a bold and audacious market move, alongside of a major market player.

The complete concept has been presented to the client. Normally, at this point, the buy order is taken and the next number is dialed. Some clients will agree to the buy order and then ask a few more questions. Perhaps they want the excited feeling to be a little warmer and fuzzier. Their question is predictable: How does this block trading really work? The broker is well versed in all pertinent and appropriate answers. For this question, he will always choose to answer why instead of how. The client usually won't pick up on the difference and enjoys hearing a story anyway.

"Block trading is the primary strategy used by the well-capitalized, professional market institutions. When these types of players want to move in or out of a position, it involves hundreds of thousands of dollars at a minimum. If the institution tried to enter a buy order of such extraordinary size, the market price would have to run up considerably to fill it. Or if such a large buy order was entered in smaller, daily increments, it could take weeks to completely execute the order. The firm takes a more efficient course. With the powerful negotiating leverage of quantity, the trader locates the other institutions with a large position in the particular stock. A transaction price is agreed upon, relative to the current market price for the shares. The selling side puts the block of shares into the market, just under the bid price. One second later, the buying side hits the bid for the shares. In one efficient move the firm has positioned into the desired stock, without impacting the current market price. When the impact does occur in the price, we want it be from the positive events our analyst anticipated. This is an example of the advantages the bigger institutions have over the individual investor. But we want our clients access to this type of advantage whenever possible."

The added bonus of a block trade is that it can be done without a commission charged to the individual account. The term *share price net to you* is used. The firm will take the spread between their bid price cost and the market ask price. This form of a markup often goes undetected, and the investor might just think it's client appreciation week.

The clients who participate in the block trade do so under one principal assumption: They are assuming the securities firm has discovered a tremendous stock market opportunity, in which they are being handed a chance to take part. That could be an acceptable premise if the commissions charged on transactions were the firm's main source of profits, but it is not. That could be an acceptable premise if the performance of the individual investor's accounts were the firm's top priority, but they are not. The firm's revenues and rewards are much more plentiful beyond the limited scope of the fees charged for executing buy and sell orders. A financial institution, engaged in the business of investment brokerage, holds its primary allegiance to its own interest, balance sheet and profit/loss statement.

The Initial Risk of the Block Trade

The firm makes its limited commitment one minute after the market opens. The predetermined stock is called up on the screen. The current price quote is displayed. The other institution holding the desired share position is contacted. The two principals quickly come to a verbal agreement. All aspects of the deal are based on where and how the stock is trading at the moment. The seller agrees to a certain relative price and the buyer nods. The buying firm is now obligated to take ownership of the entire block of shares. The actual crossing of the stock will take place just before the end of the day's trading.

Ten minutes into the market day, the firm has acquired a large position for which it will have to supply the funds due by the end of the trading day. The objective is to have the client base supply the capital required to pay for the position. The brokers are given the order. The phones start to buzz. Buy tickets begin to accumulate and are piled on the trading desk. With each increase in the ticketed buying amount, the firm is able to pass another portion of the capital commitment and market risk on to the client base. The firm does not rid itself completely of risk until the entire amount due is absorbed by the individual accounts. If this transfer of commitment is not completed by the end of trading, the unaccounted shares are paid for and are the property of the firm. And that is an unacceptable situation. The exposure to the firm must remain limited and temporary. This exposure must be quickly passed to the clients, and the potential rewards must justify the brief period of risk. For the success of any block trading scheme, the senior partner must be accurate in his benefit cost analysis.

Pass on the Risk, Keep the Commissions

There are three basic reasons that justify a brokerage firm's assumption of the initial risk of taking down a block position. The first reason is fairly up-front, and the benefits are overt. The analyst could have actually found a stock situation that appears to have some potential. Both technical and fundamental indicators point to the possibility of a price run in the next few days.

The recommendation and the research is handed to the branch manager or the senior partner. This man is in charge of the acquisition decisions. He spends a moment alone with the proposal on his desk. His mind starts to conduct the benefit-cost analysis. The benefits are plentiful. If the stock does happen to work it could be worth a lot of publicity mileage. For years to come the recommendation's results could be included in the firm's promotional materials. Perhaps the stock market is in a momentary lull. This block purchase could give the brokers something to peddle, for idle client assets do not increase anyone's production record.

This large block of shares represents a rapid influx of revenue for the firm and a feeling of goodwill for the customers. With each share moved, the firm keeps the spread and the brokers let the clients know this unique opportunity is being provided commission free. So many benefits can be had for one simple cost of assuming the risk in taking the initial stock position.

One question must be answered before accepting the risk for all the benefits. It's not whether the recommendation is well timed or if the research is sound. The one crucial consideration is if the entire block of shares can be moved into the client's accounts before the end of the trading day. If the answer is affirmative, then the green light is given. The brokers receive the order of the day and those lucky individual investors stand by for that magic phone call. The firm can express its genuine enthusiasm about that stock's potential, but does not to risk its own capital.

Preferential Treatment to the Institutional Accounts at the Expense of the Individual Accounts

The second reason behind executing a block trade demonstrates the firm's preference for the big institutional accounts over smaller individual accounts. The institutional accounts hold values well into the seven digits and are the cornerstones of the firm's total assets under management. High net worth accounts attract other big accounts and other types of business, like bringing companies public. These accounts provide the big commissions. With a single buy order, an institutional client can supply enough purchasing power to surpass that of hundreds of individual clients. The personnel assigned to service such mammoth piles of money do not mind rendering mundane types of support, like listening or giving nontransactional advice, because it is actually worth their time for these accounts.

All accounts can be the source of some degree of stress and hassle. There is nothing worse than a client who requires much more care and maintenance than the compensation justifies. The prospecting time involved in landing a big institutional account can run into several months, even years. To open the standard individual account usually requires a phone call or two. The total number of big accounts gives the firm its juice, or its influence rating. This is a vital factor determining its place in the jungle hierarchy. The roster of institutional clients is worn proudly on the sleeve of the investment firm. It shines like a badge of honor in a display of rank to the rest of the market world.

The pecking order has been established among the accounts. The interests of those in the top part of the list must be granted the higher priority. The needs of the institutional client are handled personally by one of the senior partners. So when one of these accounts needs to raise some cash, it is the man in the big corner office who gets the call.

This particular institutional client is a large real estate interest that currently holds a large stock position of a previous firm's recommendation. The spokesman for the account conveys his company's pending cash requirements for another project elsewhere. The client wants to sell the 250,000 shares of Eagle Capital that was so highly touted ten months ago. The senior partner detects a hint of frustration in the sell order, probably because the stock has not performed like the original promotion suggested. The senior partner knows he has to avoid adding insult to near injury. He has to assure the client that the net proceeds from the sell will be based on the current market price and will not be diluted from downward selling pressure. This kind of special treatment is what keeps big clients on board for future business.

The senior partner would not be able to fulfill his promise to the institutional client if he starts feeding the massive sell order into the market. This would start an overwhelming dumping momentum that would send the share price plummeting. The big customer would receive severely diminished net proceeds and probably start listening to the other firms competing for its investment business. No, that would not do.

The senior partner would not have much chance of finding another big market player to buy the block, because those guys know a bad stock when they see it. The only option available is to cross the stock within the firm's client base or move the stock from the big account into the buying demand created from the smaller accounts. This internal trade would keep the price stable and not flood the market. The institutional client would be appeased by the receipt of the complete net proceeds. The brokers would generate a dose of spread revenue for the firm and themselves, and the individual investors would be given the chance to participate in yet another unique and dynamic stock play.

The order is given to the broker corps. The numbers are dialed and the individual account holders receive the pitch. It is packaged in the usual block trading strategy format. The presentation includes the analyst's discovery of a timely opportunity and the sense of urgency. Since the transaction is to be completed in-house, the firm serves as the market maker, supplying the buyer and the seller. This enables the brokers to provide the individual clients with the added bonus of buying the stock net at the ask price without a commission. The cross is executed and the volume is reported to the appropriate exchange. Now the transaction is complete and all the parties involved have served their purpose.

The Block Trading and Private Placement Connection

The third reason that would inspire an investment firm to undertake the initial risk of block trading is potentially the most profitable. However, in some cases the rewards from this approach are both very covert and very illegal. There are a good number of publicly traded companies that do not possess the right kind of substance, or generate the proper news, to automatically attract buying interest toward their stock. Just because a public company does not have competent management, a profitable balance sheet or a decent product or service does not mean it doesn't need its share price to run up occasionally. It definitely does.

A company that has not reached the point of being profitable has one basic problem. It cannot generate enough revenue to exist independently. Some examples might be a natural resource company without a producing source of raw materials or a biotech company without a developed apparatus to sell. These companies usually do not have the net asset value on which to borrow through conventional means. Without positive cash flow or revenues, even a junk bond issue would be out of the question. The capital required to keep these publicly traded companies in business must be obtained from private sources. The preferred method is a process known as a private placement financing, which is a legal and legitimate form of raising capital. Nevertheless, there are certain circumstances when a company and a brokerage firm take this method beyond all ethical market boundaries.

Remember this term: private placement. It is crucial that this concept is fully grasped by every individual investor. When a company whose stock you are holding, finishes a private placement financing, a degree of concern is warranted. The eventual ramifications on your share price can be adverse.

Through a private placement financing, a company is going to raise operating funds from a group of private individuals. In exchange for the capital, the financiers will receive a large portion of stock from the company's treasury. The rate of exchange is very favorable for those supplying the money. If the company's stock is currently trading at a $5 bid, the typical arrangement would have the financiers give $2.50 cash, in return for each private placement share. The company takes two million shares of its own stock (current market value of $10 million) gives it to the group and receives $5 million in financing. Basically, this is two million shares of stock for 50 percent of the shares' current market value in cash. This stock will be restricted for a certain period of time before it can be sold. Depending on the situation, the restricted time period can be one day to 24 months.

But hold on a moment. If the company could get their share price up to $10, before the financing, the same arrangement would yield $10 million in operating capital. There must be some way to get that stock price up to $10 in the next month or so. This is where a corrupt retail brokerage firm enters the scene.

The retail brokerage firm has just the right tool for the job. By using its client base, the firm can supply incremental buying strength in sequential and gradually increasing doses. These doses can be administered precisely within the desired timeframe. This is just before the company is scheduled to negotiate a private placement financing. The actions required by the company and the firm must be closely coordinated.

Since the company does not have the substance to generate positive news from external sources, it must conduct its own campaign of releasing headlines to the financial media. The cooperating firm is given an advance schedule of when and what will be contained in the news releases. The firm takes the first step by circulating verbal and printed materials that portray this company as being on the verge of a meteoric rise to greatness. This goes out to the clients and hot prospects as exclusive research on a company's stock that's worth watching. The brokers pitch the first group of clients into buying some shares based on anticipated news becoming public. Perhaps the pending story involves a company acquisition or an increase in estimated earnings. The initial buyers derive a hollow feeling of comfort when they see the brokers' informative predictions come true.

Each new segment of clients who are recommended into the stock is slightly larger than the previous segment. This establishes increased buying demand. The company controlled supply of stock is held incrementally steady. Thus, the growing demand gradually overwhelms the set amount of shares available for sale at each new point on the market. If the current price quote indicates 12,000 shares offered at $6, then the next buy order comes in for 15,000 shares. The offer price then moves to $6¼. Now the bid price also moves up.

Those clients who bought earlier in the campaign are overjoyed with their new stock position that is currently on a run. The other clients, who just recently got on board, are motivated at the close coordination between the predictions at the time of purchase and the subsequent release of the relative information. With even a modest degree of smoothness, the broker can keep the clients in the shares for the "long run" and resist the temptation to take short-term profits.

This stock promotion is running at full speed. The buying strength and the trading volumes continue to increase, until the desired $10 share price is attained. The company finalizes the private placement financing. It receives its $10 million in operating capital. The financiers receive two million shares of temporarily restricted stock with a current market value of $20 million. The shareholders are left holding a position at a time that usually proves to be very disadvantageous. On the horizon, a huge amount of cheap stock is waiting to be sold, and gravity can substantially affect the share price when the hype moves elsewhere.

The Covert Reward on the Dark Side of Block Trades and Private Placements

The investment firm will demand a high price for its role in the stock promotion. A client base can only take so much abuse in any given year. Although this type of block trading angle is the most lucrative for the firm, it can also result in the most drastic losses in individual client account values. It is an emotional roller coaster for the clients involved. They see their share price start to run and experience the barrage of hype and media promotion. Then, they watch the gains crumble into losses caused by the events of postpromotion syndrome. The firm and its brokers become the recipients of the bitter fruits of the clients resultant frustration and despair. For all this, the firm demands substantial payment.

During the promotion of Eagle Capital stock, the share price moved from $5 up to $10. The total block of stock that the firm recommended to its clients was 250,000 shares at an average price of 8¼ per share. The total amount of client funds put into the stock during the promotion was $2,062,500. The firm charged the company 20 percent of that amount, or $412,500. The payment was made under the table and tax-free. It was a very profitable arrangement for both players. The company just received $5 million in operating capital and sold cheap stock out of its treasury during the run from $5 to $10. The payment to the cooperating firm was yet another great short-term investment.

Beyond the initial risk of the involvement in a blatantly illegal endeavor, the firm's rewards are threefold. The first is the convenience of almost a half million dollars in nonreportable income without the nuisance of taxation.

The second reward is comprised of all the commissions charged on the initial buy side and again on the eventual sell side. However, the firm could take this opportunity to show the clients how much they are appreciated. Since there is such a big covert payoff, giving the customers a little break on transaction fees could be justified.

The third rewarding aspect is the multiplication of each account's intrinsic value to the firm. Even those with smaller asset values have become worthwhile. The typical small account does approximately three trades a year, for a maximum total of $10,000 principal involved. Over the table, that represents gross revenue of $300 for the whole year, which is split among the house, the broker, the exchange and the tax man. This hardly pays for the time and trouble related to actually servicing the client. But with block trading's covert rewards, even the small account is seen in a new light. One of the account's three annual trades involves about $3,300 dollars. The house might give a small break on the commission, because now, with just one trade, the account is bringing in almost $700 in net cash.

The brokers, who work these types of covert compensation stock plays, refer to them as special dividend stocks or stock with a back-end load. Even if they were given a choice, the brokers would work these plays anyway. They figure most of the firm's recommendations are going to go down, so they might as well make some decent money beforehand.

This type of block trading promotional situation is much more prevalent than anyone in the industry realizes or wants to admit. In the same sense that even ugly dogs need love, marginal companies need to have buying strength move their shares prices, from time to time. The preceding arrangement between the company and the investment firm is necessary to attract investors' attention and to create the required buying strength, although it is fundamentally undeserved.

Regardless of a firm's particular block trading strategy, the underlying principles of such an action are the same. Dissecting the event reveals what has actually happened. A particular stock position was determined to hold some intrinsic reward value. The rewards from this position are realized only by creating new capital commitment to the stock. This commitment must be done in a fashion that maintains or adds temporary buying strength to the share price. For whatever motive, the targeted stock is going to be moved from an institution, through a retail firm, and out to a vast number of individual client accounts. The investment firm is the catalyst. It provides a contrived demand, as a home for the supply. For the first few moments of the transaction, the firm puts its own capital at risk. Within a few hours, the firm has redistributed that risk to its individual client base.

A block of stock has been moved from a large institution to a number of smaller investors. The needs of the firm, the publicly traded company and the large institutional investment account have all been served by this block trading endeavor. Their rewards are immediate and any risk incurred is only temporary. The individual investor is left at a complete disadvantage. The individual client's recent purchase of the particular stock is merely a hollow sense of urgency emanating from a biased source.

Individual Self-Defense Against the Block Trade

Before I present the next way you lose money on your way to the stock market, I want to offer a few tips related to block trading. My message regarding this subject is simple. Individual investors should never allow their capital to participate in a block trade. Of the three parties involved in this transaction, the individual investor is the one that gets taken. The individual investor provides the money and endures all the risk, while the other two parties take the immediate reward. The investor is now the proud owner of a stock that does not possess a high success percentage. Other market players, who truly understand, love to short these stocks after such block trades occur.

The individual clients should consider their firm to be part of the competition. The broker works for an entity primarily concerned with the returns in its own stock account. If an investment firm buys a block of stock that's really on the verge of a price run, why should it let the small accounts in on it? Commissions are not the main source of a firm's profitability.

When presented with a block trade opportunity, the source of the recommendation must be properly considered, as well as the needs of the institution being served on the other side of that source. Know your role in the triangle of a block trade.

The privileged roles are always reserved for the institutions. When the client receives the pitch to participate in a block trade, it creates a "missing the boat" feeling. This feeling can be the cause of a bad investment decision. A much higher rate of success goes to those who wait and watch the particular stock for 3 to 5 days. Block traded stocks, even the ones that temporarily move up in value, are subject to steep price declines immediately after the transaction. Those who wait until just after the redistribution of capital and risk can expect a much better purchase price.

Your mission in a block trade, should you decide to accept it, is to provide your money as a means to someone else's end. You'll receive all the disadvantages of a precarious position and unfair odds for your efforts. This mission is the catalyst for the 11th way you lose money on your way to the stock market.

WAY #11: *When a broker gives you the opportunity to participate in his firm's block trade, seize the moment, for you are among the fortunate ones who the broker was able to contact that day.* The investment firm has demonstrated a gesture of true altruism by this sudden invitation. There must have been countless fortunes made in a panic and without considerate thought, right?

CHAPTER 7

The Good and Bad Breeds of Stock Splits

The Ways You Lose: 12

The Stock Split as a Barometer

A company's stock follows a unique path of development throughout its market life. The price direction taken by the shares isn't always directly related to the successful operation of the underlying corporate entity. There are outstanding companies with poorly performing stocks due entirely to external aspects. A dismal share price could be caused by retaining untalented promoters, being traded by incompetent specialists or market makers or existing within an obscure and misunderstood industrial sector. Bringing constructive attention to a certain stock are the traditional catalyst for upward price movement. Thus, a publicly traded company's structural strength and the quality of its stock are not necessarily reflective of one another.

However, the event known as a stock split does mirror the current status of a particular company. A negative or a positive reflection is based on the type of split being implemented on the stock. According to this type of split, the upcoming share price direction can be projected within a high degree of probable accuracy. Investment decision competence is strengthened through understanding the underlying forces within the market. In order to be enlightened about reverse splits and their ramifications, you need to start with a conceptual view.

The Good Type of Stock Split

A stock split can either increase or decrease the number of shares outstanding. The individual shareholders usually do not realize a split is implemented until after the fact. Notification is often in the form of the monthly statement. Somewhere in the account activity section, there is a representative entry of the transition. The original share amount has been increased or decreased, but the overall market value has not changed, for the time being. The clients who do take notice of the split rarely comprehend why it happened, what type of split occurred or what were the underlying causes. This is another classic example of how the majority of individual investors allow events to happen to them, while relying on a strategy of merely hoping for the best.

The good type of stock split is the one in the standard format. A certain share issue is currently trading at $60. Notification is released that the company intends to implement a 3-for-1 split on its shares. That means every share at $60 will become three shares at $20 each, after the split. If an investor holds 1,000 presplit shares at $6,000 total market value, then his postsplit position will be 3,000 shares at the same $6,000 total market value. Although the number of shares owned has increased, and the current price per share has decreased, each shareholder has maintained his overall percentage of ownership in the company.

This standard type of split usually originates from a position of strength. A company whose shares have experienced a sustained period of upward momentum will institute a stock split as a means to prolong any forward progress. As overwhelming buying interest continues to drive a stock upward, it eventually reaches a point where the investing public begins to feel the price has become too lofty. Many institutions and individuals are now content to just hold tight and not buy, or add to their positions. If the previous buying interest is allowed to diminish, it could mean an end to the climbing share price.

The company responds with the implementation of a stock split. Overall share positions are multiplied and the price per share is now down to a level where the current upward momentum started. The new, lower share price appears more appetizing to the investing public, especially for the stock of such a high caliber company. The company continues to attract buying interest to its shares. New positions are established and previous positions are increased. The upward price trend resumes.

In general terms, this standard split is healthy for all those involved, especially before the transition. Whether the particular stock is of blue chip status and has climbed gradually over a period of years, such as Motorola, or is a newer issue, such as Snapple, which shot up drastically upon its initial public offering, the mutual benefits of the split are similar.

The presplit shareholders usually experience continued growth of equity in their original investment, as the newcomers jump on board. The company keeps the momentum going without diluting its own percentage of ownership in the outstanding shares. But this time, if the upward price trend continues, the company will increase its market capitalization by whatever multiple of the original stock split.

For instance, in presplit status, the company has 20 million shares outstanding, a current share price of $50, and a total market capitalization of $1 billion. After a 2-for-1 stock split, there are 40 million shares outstanding, a new share price of $25 but the same market capitalization, for the time being. With the high probability of continued, upward price movement, it is reasonable to project a $50 share price in the future. If the stock does eventually climb back to $50, the new market capitalization will be $2 billion. It is important to remember this split did not dilute anyone's percentage of ownership in the outstanding shares. And with this increase in capitalization, the stock option and warrant plans that benefit the corporate insiders become even more lucrative.

The key to the standard stock split is that continued attraction of buying interest can keep the share price moving up. A stock on the verge of splitting is usually doing so from a position of strength. For those individuals holding or considering buying such a stock, there is a high degree of probability for a profitable investment experience. At the very least, holding or buying a stock on the verge of this kind of split is *not* one of those obvious and avoidable premarket decision mistakes.

Which brings us to the other side of this stock split coin. This is the evil twin of the above transition. The reverse split comes from a much different angle and is fraught with harsher realities and pitfalls. A defining look at the origins, the purpose and the possible ulterior motives related to reverse stock splits will reveal why they have long been a source of monetary losses for the investing public.

The Bad Type of Stock Split

The reverse stock split functions as its name implies. A company's stock currently trades at $1. The company implements a 1-for-5 reverse stock split. Every five shares of presplit stock is amalgamated into one share. The new stock price, immediately after the split, is $5. The investor, who had previously held 1,000 shares, is now the proud owner of 200 shares of the postsplit stock. The current market value of the position, before and after the reverse split, is $1,000.

From this brief and definitive view, one might form the opinion that reverse splits do not seem so bad. True, the investor now holds less shares, but no market value or percentage of ownership has been lost in the transition. The higher share price, with a much smaller amount of stock in the public float, gives the position an air of scarcity and improved quality.

The shareholder does not suffer a loss of asset value or a dilution of ownership value upon completion of this rollback of shares outstanding. But this equality is usually very temporary. Shortly after the reverse stock split, its underlying harsh realities begin to take their toll on the new share price. These new shares, incidentally, are now mainly in the hands of individual investors. For various reasons, the institutions that had sizable positions in the prereverse split stock had no interest in continuing their involvement after the transition. The inhabitants of the market jungle are rarely convinced by a reverse split's cosmetic camouflage of the stock's true situation.

Before we increase the depth of our examination, let me dispel a related and popular myth. The act of splitting a stock, whatever the direction, is not a decision made solely by the company's board of directors. Technically, approval must be granted by the majority of the shareholders. Through some news medium capacity, the company will announce its proposal to implement a stock split. The date and location of the pertinent shareholder meeting is set. For all those who cannot attend, the company will mail out proxy forms, with which shareholders can cast their vote. Once the input from the meeting and the mail are totaled, the split proposal is carried out or rejected, accordingly.

Although this process appears to be ostensibly democratic, the outcome is almost always decided before the vote is ever taken. There is usually a degree of individual shareholder disgruntlement. Especially if the stock split is in the reverse direction. I have spoken with many enraged investors who demanded their particular shares not be included in the reverse split. Of course, such demands always go unheeded. Not that these people understood the inherent down side to such endeavors, but their anger was based on the dissatisfaction of owning less share than before. Regardless of the type of proposed split, its approval is predetermined. The votes of the individual shareholders do not have a deciding impact, because this group never comprises the majority of shareholders. The bulk of the outstanding shares are held in the company's treasury, or with closely aligned institutions and institutionally sized shareholders. The votes representing this stock will be cast in favor of management's proposals.

While shareholder votes are mere formalities, an individual investor's personal involvement is self-determined. If this individual is aware of the pending action and is aware of the relative ramifications, then a knowledgeable decision to buy, sell or hold can be made. Instead of the individual allowing some unfathomable market occurrence to just happen, this person can become enlightened to the ways of the market. The individual investor can break losing traditions by making informed market decisions and pursuing a structured investment formula.

The Reverse Split as Presented to the Investing Public

Another subject that needs to be covered is the avoidance of stocks in the midst of reverse split activity. I have touted the potential of many such stocks in my time. Technically, the benefits projected in my recommendations were genuine. But there is a general market rule that, of the two parties involved in any market transaction, one side has the advantageous angle and the ulterior motive. One side is the recipient of the immediate rewards of the transaction and the other side endures the risk and uncertainty. This general market rule applies directly to reverse stock splits. The advantage goes to the market insider, the company and its institutional allies. This one-sided scenario begins when the idea of a reverse stock split is first presented to the investing public.

As with any other aspect of the stock market, there is a substantial difference in a reverse split's presentation to investors and its underlying reality. If such a split is pending, the subject will rarely be included in any related promotional material. The brokerage firm, charged with the self-serving duties of attracting buying interest to a particular company's stock, will not have its brokers begin their pitch with "It's a unique opportunity to buy a piece of a company on the verge of explosive growth and a reverse stock split."

The interested investment firm does not try to avoid or hide the issue of the pending reverse split. It's just best not to draw attention to such things. It meets the occasional objection or challenge with a prepared response. Promotional personnel, whether it be a broker, financial news journalist or a seminar host, can shed an acceptable light on anything. The appropriate routine is held in the reserve script arsenal. When the need arises, the routine is simply added to the end of the specific stock script.

There are three standard points presented in the routine. The first is the ideal of neutrality. The pending reverse split is initially portrayed to have neutral consequences. The 1,000 shares at $1 will simply become 200 shares at $5, after the 1-for-5 reverse split. There will be no change in the value of the position, and there will be no dilution of percentage ownership of shares. This primary point emphasizes a basic message: Reverse stock splits are a common occurrence, and there is nothing to worry about.

The second point is presented, if the first point fails to satisfy the concerns of the inquiring investor. The second point extols the benefit of the reverse split as an effective way to reduce the number of shares outstanding. If the pending reverse split is set at 1-for-5, then a public float of 20 million shares would quickly become 4 million. With a smaller, more manageable amount of shares outstanding, the company's market capitalization and stock price can move higher from less buying power. This point stretches the idea that something can become more valuable, if it merely becomes scarcer.

The third point that defends the virtue of reverse stock splits packages the transition as a bit of market strategy. The reverse split will be presented as an actual buying interest magnet. It is conceivable, under certain circumstances, a stock price would start to rally as a result of a recent reverse split. However, certain factors would have to be present before the most imaginative market professional would even consider presenting this third point.

The prereverse split stock price must have been below $5 per share. The postreverse split stock price must be above $5 per share, at least for a short time. For example, a stock at $4 per share undergoes a reverse split of 1-for-4. It opens the following day at $16. All these shareholders now own one-fourth of the stock than before, but its new, loftier price instantly allows greater buying capacity through leverage. Once a stock attains a market price above $5, it can be put on margin and provide a credit line to buy more of the stock. This point assumes the margined masses will still want to buy the shares and the price will remain above $5 long enough to allow leveraged purchases. The broker knows its believability greatly depends on the gullibility and the ignorance of his particular audience.

These points regarding reverse split benefits are contrived and misconstrued. The possible redeeming qualities might seem shallow and improbable, but these concepts work quite well in soothing the concerns of an unwary investing public. This soft packaging of the remote rewards does nothing to help cushion the blunt reality of the eventual consequences of such splits.

As an individual investor buying or holding a stock on the verge of a reverse split, you must remember that the prospects for success deteriorate the moment the transition is complete. There is no monetary gain. The preservation of overall asset value is temporary. Shareholders suddenly inherit a very precarious position. Their stock, now of a newly reduced outstanding share amount, is ripe for a secondary offering of more shares by the company. This action has a magnified, diluting effect on shareholders' original percentage interest in the company. Additionally, the reverse split, accompanied by an immediately higher share price on a lower amount of shares, requires greater price movement for the position to realize a profit.

Postreverse Split Pitfalls

Consider the problem of magnified dilution. The company's shares, currently trading at $1 with 20 million shares outstanding, undergo a reverse split of 1-for-5. The new current market price is $5 and the new amount of shares outstanding is 4 million. If the company acts fast, it can raise a substantial sum of additional market capital. This could be accomplished with a secondary stock offering. With the higher share price and the reduced public share float, there is timely reason and room for such an endeavor. If the company decides to issue more shares into the market, it will be at the peril of the current shareholders. The immediate and certain rewards will go exclusively to the company.

If the size of the secondary offering is 2 million shares at the current market price of $5, the company will gross a lump sum of $10 million. Stock offerings are the ultimate way of raising capital. A secondary stock offering is a transaction that heavily favors the company. It trades a pile of intangible stock certificates for a pile of very tangible money. This exchange of illuminated paper for the investment funds of the masses is much more advantageous than borrowing from a bank or issuing a bond. The pieces of illuminated paper do not charge interest nor require the backing of any real assets.

The secondary stock offering situation is not so rosy for the original, prereverse split shareholders. Their percentage of ownership in the company will endure a magnified degree of dilution the moment the new shares hit the market. The market value of their original investment is also put in further jeopardy.

The shareholder's original position was 1,000 shares at $1 of a 20-million-share float. After the reverse split of 1-for-5, the new position is 200 shares at $5 of a 4-million-share float. A secondary offering of 2 million shares at $5 requires the original shareholder to purchase 100 shares of the new issue to maintain a percentage ownership in the company. If the shareholder decides not to buy additional shares, the original position percentage will become diluted, and this is the point where that dilution becomes magnified, because not only has the amount of his or her original shares been rolled back, but also new shares are being added to the public float at five times the original price.

It makes no monetary difference to the company. It raises its capital from the market by the number of shares being offered, at whatever the current price. The funds are placed in the company treasury. The public float amount will remain constant and the share price will fluctuate. But the catch is that the share price will fluctuate in the hands of the shareholders. The company's objective for the secondary offering has yielded the desired capital, and the risk has been transferred to the shareholders. The exchange of certificates for money has served the company well. The shareholders must endure the risk and worry of pursuing profits in an uncertain market.

This pursuit of profits becomes more perilous with the higher postreverse split share price and the addition of more shares from the secondary offering. It is a matter of the distance a stock has to move up, and the resistance it has to move through, to provide a profit for the investor. At the prereverse split price of $1, the stock would need to move up at least 25 cents, within a year, to make the risk and fees begin to pay off. The postreverse split position at $5 would have to move up to at least $1, before acceptable net profits could be realized. Although the percentage of advance is the same, success in the prereverse split stock scenario is more probable. The stock, at $1, requires less buying strength to reach its primary profit objective, than its postreverse split and postsecondary offering counterpart.

This counterpart stock needs to move from $5 to $6 per share. The required $1 move is a tough psychological obstacle, especially with the recently increased number of shares, that could suddenly turn into intensified selling pressure from a jittery new mass of shareholders. The one point jump is unlikely because of the reluctance of institutional buying interest to move into postreverse split stock. This reluctance is inspired by the knowledge and vision of the entities that dwell in the market jungle. The market institutions can clearly see the red flags and steer clear of stocks on the verge of reverse splits.

The Direction of Split in Direct Relation to Current Status of the Company

The warning signs are quite clear. The individual investor must be attentive or risk another mistake. If a person were to invest with any forethought, he or she would avoid reverse split stocks on general principles. The first of these principles relates to the situations that inspire a company to implement a reverse split on its own stock.

When a publicly traded company rolls back its outstanding share float, it does so from a position of weakness. This status becomes apparent after a simple comparison of two different companies planning to implement stock splits. The first company will do a standard split of 3-for-1. For one share of its stock at $60, the shareholders will have three shares at $20. This company has a common denominator with other corporate entities in similar situations. For any company about to do a standard split to its stock, things are usually going well. The business operations are profitable and growing, and the shares are performing in an upward and steady manner.

The situation is not the same for the second company, on the verge of a reverse stock split. This company's operations and stock are going the opposite direction of the first company. The second company will roll back its stock at a rate of 1-for-4. Four shares at $5 will now be one share at $20. This company joins the dismal ranks of the other corporations proposing the same transition. It is very rare to find a company that is experiencing good times, both in business operations and stock performance, that is also implementing a reverse stock split. If one of these companies really wanted to reduce its amount of outstanding shares, they would start to buy them from the market. If these companies were fundamentally worthy of the buying interest, that would run their share prices up, and they would not have to artificially push the stock forward with a reverse split.

Whatever the ulterior motive for the company to roll back its share float, the immediate benefits will go to the company and the supporting players of the transaction. Upon completion of the reverse split, the risk is transferred to the individual shareholders. They endure the uncertainties of holding a stock that the company and the institutions wouldn't touch. The individual shareholders will be the ones to experience magnified dilution should a secondary offering follow the reverse split. It is a one-sided venture from the start. All the advantage is held by those who operate on the inside. Regardless of how visible this uneven playing field can be before the transition, multitudes of individual investors chose to play the role of sucker in pending reverse stock splits. This type of highly probable hardship is completely preventable. With that thought in mind, I present the 12th way you lose money, by way of reverse stock splits.

WAY #12: *Buy and hold stocks that are in the midst of implementing a reverse split.* The negative underlying causes and ramifications are not as important as the instantly higher share price, immediately after the transaction. And higher share prices is the name of the investment game.

CHAPTER 8

Why Margin Accounts Prohibit Investment Success

The Ways You Lose: 13 and 14

The Inevitable Encounter with the Concept of Margin

It can happen on the day the account is opened or at a strategically chosen moment down the road. The broker will implore the client to convert his cash account into a margin account. There are two schools of thought among the broker corps. One side will introduce the idea on the first day of the relationship. The other side will use certain positive market events to justify the conversion.

In its presented form, a margin account seems like a good deal for everyone. The typical introduction scenario involves some standard supporting arguments. The first would be a reference to a recent upward push in the broader markets: perhaps the Dow Jones Industrial Average reaches a new high. The second reference would be to one of the firm's stock recommendations that happened to be up a few points, since the broker had first mentioned it. The third supporting argument is the idea of achieving a higher level of investing sophistication. The following broker pitch is often used to compel the client to convert to a margin account.

"Good morning Mr. Sanders, I wanted to touch base with you about some positive developments. As mentioned in the financial news on Friday, all the major indexes closed at their highs for the year, as did the trading volume on the New York. And in case you hadn't noticed,

79

Cal Fed Bank is performing quite well. You might remember, when I pointed it out three weeks ago, it was trading at $20. Well it closed on Friday at 22½. What this means is that the current market has all the classic indicators of a major price run, in the immediate future. Now it's obvious this firm knows what it's doing. So you and I need to ensure the account is in the proper position to take full advantage of the pending market run. There are a couple of companies that our analysts have targeted for explosive growth. And now is the time to take share positions, while we're in the early stages of a bull market."

At this point, clients will often anticipate the broker's suggestion of either adding money to the account or liquidating a current position to create the funds for further investment. Some clients will have prepared objections ready to rattle off, when the broker stops talking. But the experienced storyteller knows how to circumvent these possible road blocks.

"Now Mr. Sanders, I don't think this is the time to add any more funds to the account, nor should we sell any of our current positions. If I could make a suggestion? (Wait for response.) The best way to ensure we get the most mileage and performance from the current portfolio is to convert to a margin account. Today's market value of the positions we now hold gives us an additional $25,000 of buying power. I'll fax you the margin agreement right now, and I'll mail the originals for you to sign and send back. Account services will put the account on margin today, so we can start trading on a higher level immediately. This is how the institutions operate in the stock market. They increase their capacity to buy into bull markets, by using their current positions to expand their purchasing strength. An information booklet on margin accounts is being mailed with the rest of the material. Anyway, let me cover the details of the two stock positions that we need to consider today. . ."

And so an account is transformed. The client's current securities are used as the anchor to provide a credit line for further investment. For the firm and its brokers, margin accounts are a great deal. Some simple paperwork and a few keystrokes on the computer are all that is required. Once on margin, a client's trading activity is increased in size and frequency. Bigger trades, and more often, can mean greater commissions. Depending on the type of securities being used to anchor the credit line, every dollar added to a margin account actually represents $1.50 to $1.80 that can be used for further investment. The most important aspect, to the firm, is the addition of more market muscle.

Every account on margin gives the firm increased buying strength that can be focused into a particular stock in times of need.

For the retail client, the miracle of margin account investing can be a different story. If all goes well all the time, the individual investor, trading on margin, will do just fine. But even the novice should know involvement in numerous, consecutive and successful market endeavors has a low percentage of probability. It's all part of the curse of being an uninformed client. However, there are some constants throughout the margined client's experience. Here are a few:

- The margined client will pay interest charges on the amount of the credit line being utilized.

- The margined client will have to add money or liquidate positions, should the market value of the anchor securities drop below a certain level.

- Margined clients will have a much harder time trying to determine the actual net value of their account.

- Margined clients will become involved in trading well beyond their normal monetary capacity.

In market terms, margined clients are investing beyond their realistic means.

Clearing the Fog of Margin Through Comparative Observation

Margin accounts are confusing, which is by the design of those who dwell within the market jungle. A trip through the typical working scenario of an individual's margin account experience, compared with another individual's regular account experience, should clear some of the conceptual clouds.

Let's start with two clients who are considering investing on margin. Both clients begin with a cash or regular investment account. Both accounts contain identical portfolios. The current market value of each account is $50,000. The common stock position has a market value of $25,000. The account also contains a block of AAA rated, insured, municipal bonds issued by a county government in southern

California. The bonds are at their face value of $25,000. The stock is exchange traded within the United States, and trades at over $5 per share, thus qualifying it to be margined against. The municipal bonds also qualify to be an anchor for a margin account. The word *anchor* is being used to represent those securities being margined or borrowed against to buy more securities.

The clients receive the standard pitch for account conversion. One client agrees to switch to a margin account. The other client decides to maintain his regular account.

For margin investment purposes, the $25,000 worth of common stock creates $12,500 of buying power. The $25,000 worth of municipal bonds adds an additional $20,000 line of investing credit. The percentage that can be margined off the municipal bonds is higher than for stocks, because this type of debt instrument is considered to be more conservative and stable. In total, this $50,000 portfolio can be margined to provide $32,500, for additional investment.

The client who opted for margin decides to use $25,000 worth of the new buying power. The interest charged on margin accounts fluctuates with the rest of the rates. For this example, I'll use 8 percent. The $25,000 line of credit, or debit, will cost $2,000 over a year's time. The broker recommends the client's current stock positions should be increased. The client agrees and $25,000 is added to the stock side of the portfolio. For this example, I'll assume the broker is giving the client a preferred commission rate of 4 percent. The commission costs going into the additional stock positions are $1,000.

This client is now considered to be leveraged. The objective for the next year is to achieve a substantial net return, beyond interest charges, commissions, taxes and the outstanding debit balance. This newly margined portfolio starts with a market value of $75,000, and a debit balance of $25,000. The purchase of the additional stock and the interest charges have a total cost of $3,000. There are three possible results to this account's next year of life: positive, flat, or negative at year end. For the leveraged client, determining the net return is much more complicated than merely checking relative share prices.

To Margin or Not To Margin in a Good Year

Starting with an optimistic attitude dictates that our first consideration will be of a positive performance year. The next 365 days is a period of stable interest rates and solid, steady growth in the broader market indexes. The price on the $25,000 of insured, tax-free municipal bonds holds its value and pays its annual yield of 5¾ percent. This portion of the portfolio brings in $1,438.

During this year of positive performance, the equity side of the portfolio brings in impressive numbers. The average return of the stock position is 20 percent. The stock portion of the account that was worth $50,000 on day one is now ending the year valued at $60,000. The interest yield from the bonds is tax-free and goes into the account's cash fund. The total value of the leveraged portfolio is $86,438, with a debit balance of $25,000. The client decides to pay off the debit balance and take the year's profits off the table. Now $35,000 worth of stock will have to be sold. Assuming the broker is kind enough to sell it for 3 percent, the liquidation will cost $1,050. Capital gains tax in the 28 percent bracket will be $9,800. Add up the debit balance, the taxes, the buy and sell commissions and the interest charges, and the total cost for maintaining the margin account for a year was $38,850.

When the smoke clears, the leveraged client begins to see the net return. His regular account, valued at $50,000, was margined up to $75,000. At year end, interest and capital gains put the leveraged account value at $86,438. Subtract the year's total costs of $38,850, and the net result is $47,588.

In a good year, the leveraged client actually realized a $2,412 loss on the original $50,000. Proponents of margin accounts could argue that the client would not be obligated to pay off the debit balance at the end of the first year, and thus would not have to pay off $9,800 in capital gains tax or $1,050 in sell commissions. This is true. However, the leveraged client would then run the risk of the market values dropping on the positions in the portfolio, and he would continue to be charged interest on the debit balance.

The nonleveraged client experienced the same market year and maintained regular status on the account. Her results were profitable. With the stable interest rates and tax-free income yield, accompanied by the 20 percent growth on the stock side, the nonleveraged portfolio would end the year at $56,438 in value. The client decides to take profits on the stock price gains, and assuming the broker charges the same rate of 3 percent, the liquidation costs would be $150. Capital gains tax would be $1,400. Without margin, this identically positioned account, enjoying the same positive market year, would have a total cost of $1,550. The net gain on the nonleveraged portfolio is $4,888 on the original $50,000.

To Margin or Not To Margin in a Flat Year

If the year had seen flat markets and the same margin account broke even in asset value, the client would probably hold the positions. The leveraged client's total cost, for the margined stock purchases and interest charges, would be $3,000 for the year. There would continue to be interest charges for the $25,000 debit balance outstanding. This margin account would receive an interest yield of $1,438, but subtract the costs, and the leveraged client would realize a year end loss of $1,562. Compare this with the nonleveraged client, who during this flat market year would come away with a net yield of $1,438.

To Margin or Not To Margin in a Bad Year

The leveraged client stands to take the biggest losses during the negative market periods. Consider the original account. It contains $25,000 of stocks and $25,000 of a municipal bond issue, from a county in southern California. The stocks can be margined up to 50 percent of market value. The municipal bonds can be margined up to 80 percent. This combined portfolio allows for a 65 percent margin against its assets. The client has chosen to utilize $25,000 of credit line against the $50,000 current asset value. He is margined at 50 percent.

On day one, the $25,000 debit balance is 50 percent of the anchor securities' current market value. With this particular combination of anchor securities, the debit balance cannot become more than 65 percent of their current market value. If this happens, a margin call will result. The leveraged client will be required to either add more money or liquidate a certain value amount of securities. The funds would have to be used to pay down the debit balance, so that it is below the 65 percent limitation. This is a very important point, since we are about to enter a down year in the market.

Our leveraged client begins his year. He has $50,000 of stocks and $25,000 in municipal bonds, with a 50 percent debit balance of $25,000. On day one, the total value of this margin account is $75,000. Our nonleveraged client begins her year with a regular account. She maintains the original $25,000 of stock and $25,000 of the municipal bond issue. Her first day market value is $50,000 of non-margined securities.

During the first six months of the year, the market and these port-folios hold relatively steady. Thus far, the leveraged client has paid $1,000 in interest charges, and another $1,000 in commissions, when he purchased the additional stock on margin. The leveraged client has received $719 in municipal bond yield, but is still down $1,281 at the year's half-way point. The nonleveraged client is up $719.

In the seventh month, the market takes some nasty turns. Interest rates begin to rise slightly. There are negative news releases pertaining to the company whose stock is in the two portfolios. A dose of selling pressure hits the stock and the bonds. The price drops are substantial, but not complete disasters. By the end of this month, the market stabi-lizes and the smoke clears. The stock dropped 12 percent, bonds dropped 10 percent in market value. For the leveraged client, his current, overall account value is at $66,500. His debit balance is still $25,000, and with the lower value of his anchor securities at $44,500, he is currently margined at 56 percent, but still under his limit. However, he was charged another month of interest on the debit balance. The nonleveraged client is down the same percentage, but did not have to pay any interest.

The year moves towards the end of its ninth month. The leveraged client pays another two months of interest charges. More negative developments hit the news wire. Interest rates jump up again. The county that issued the municipal bonds declares bankruptcy. County officials say its due to massive losses in the county's institutionally managed investment account. The situation becomes worse when the company, whose stock is in the portfolios, reports revenue losses for the third quarter.

The municipal bonds, although insured in regards to interest pay-ments, drop 35 percent from their market values at the beginning of the year. The new environment of rising interest rates and negative earning reports causes broad and specific sector market selling. The stock portion of the portfolios comes off 40 percent, from the market values at the beginning of the year. The nonleveraged client is down $18,750 or 38 percent, from her original $50,000 investment. All that she can really do, and all that is required of her at the moment is to ride out this slide in the market.

During these dark market moments, much more is required of the leveraged client. The overall value of his portfolio drops to $46,250 from the original $75,000. His debit balance is still at $25,000, but now his anchor securities have a total value of $31,250, which means his margin rate is at 80 percent, well beyond the limit. The leveraged client is contacted by his firm and informed that a margin call is being made on his account. He must reduce the size of his debit balance until it is below 65 percent of the current value of the anchor securities. The leveraged client is given two options. He can deposit $5,000 in cash and pay the debit balance down to the required level, or he could liquidate $5,000 in securities to meet the obligatory reduction in the debit balance.

The leveraged client is shaken by the impact of all the negative market developments. He is hesitant to throw more money into such an uncertain environment. He is also financially overextended. He chooses the option to liquidate securities. On the first day of the tenth month, the leveraged client sells $5,000 of stock to pay down his debit balance, below the maximum limit. One bit of good fortune, the portfolio did not drop any further, and there were no more margin calls for the remainder of the year.

As the dust settled at the end of a disastrous year, the leveraged client was able to assess the damage. From day one to the six month mark, and after margined buying commissions and debit balance interest charges, minus positive bond yield, he was down $1,281. Up to the last day of the ninth month, the leveraged client paid another $500 in interest charges and was down $28,750 in total account value. The first day of the tenth month, he sold stock to meet his margin call and paid $310 in commissions. His new debit balance was $20,000. He paid $400 more in interest charges for the last three months of the year.

So on day one the leveraged client had a margin account valued at $75,000, with a debit balance of $25,000. On day 365, his margin account value is at $43,759. The total loss was $31,241 or 42 percent. And the leveraged client still has a debit balance of $20,000, on which he will continue to pay interest charges, until it is paid off. If the debit balance is added to the total loss, then the leveraged client lost more money then he originally started with, before he put himself on margin.

The nonleveraged client also had a pretty rough year. Her account finished at $31,969, down from $50,000 for a total loss of $18,031 or 36 percent. She didn't have to sell stock at a time of market weakness.

She could hang on to her entire portfolio through this rough market period. Best of all, she did not lose borrowed money and does not have an outstanding debt to pay off, and on which to pay interest.

The message of these previous examples should be clear. Whether the market year is moderately good, flat, or a bit on the rough side, it is not in the individual investor's best interest to put himself on margin. The concept of margin compels the clients to assume market commitments beyond their normal fiscal means. They are fronted capital that obligates them for much more and much longer than they had intended. If things go well, the benefits to the client are tainted due to the hidden fees and costs of leverage. If things go poorly, the ill effects are greatly magnified. Margin is the shovel by which investors can dig the hole and bury themselves. The most frightening aspect of those who push the idea of margin investing is that they look to profit from the damaging effects other peoples' excesses.

Margin's Checkered Past

The lessons learned from margin account investing have varying degrees of severity. Most of these lessons are learned at the expense of the individual client. However, the biggest disaster of margin investing once affected an entire nation. The abuses were rampant and the costs were high. A country saw the catalyst of its economy quickly brought to its knees. The ramifications were devastating and lasted for more than a decade.

The darkest spot in the checkered past of margin investing was the stock market crash of 1929. The time period preceding this event was one of fast-paced excess in many areas of American society. This was especially true on Wall Street. The buying frenzy was sending the indexes to unrealistic highs for that moment in history. Forces behind this rampant bull market were coming from artificial means. At its peak, the stock market was leveraged beyond its hilt. The cause was quite basic. There were no real limitations on margin trading. Regardless of an investor's size or underlying asset base, enormous credit lines could be obtained, with relatively minuscule amounts of cash and securities being used as the anchor. Four thousand dollars of stocks could be margined to create $16,000 of buying power. And $200,000 of underlying assets could be the anchor for a million dollar portfolio. Individuals and institutions were entrenched in stock positions that were four and five times beyond their normal capacities. Share price increases raced at speeds matched only by the lines of credit being offered. Nobody noticed when the zenith was reached, and nobody thought it would end.

History is quite clear on this point. The end came with such destructive force that the entire planet was knocked into economic depression, a depression so deep that a two-ton tablet of Prozac would not have helped. The crash of 1929 was a shining example of how periods of panic buying and periods of panic selling will each end and replace each other. The times in between these two interchanging periods are those of monotonous and moderately fluctuating markets.

The beginning of the end occurred at the point of complete buying saturation. It was as if everyone who was going to join the buying frenzy had already done so. All involved were sitting at maximum leverage and were strapped in for what they thought would be a continuing ride to riches. However, the market run peaked and retraced slightly. The market values of portfolios all dropped a notch, but the enormous debit balances stayed the same.

The first round of margin calls went out. The majority of investors were not holding cash, so they elected to sell stock in order to meet their margin requirements. This started a selling frenzy that would quickly grow to mammoth proportions. There was no more buying strength to meet even the initial amount of selling pressure. Share prices continued to drop. The number of margin calls increased. Without cash or further purchasing power, investors had no choice but to continue to sell stock. Share prices and the indexes were in a free fall. Margin calls could no longer be met. Securities that were backing the proportionately outrageous credit lines fell to a fraction of their previous values or stopped trading all together.

The majority of individual and institutional investors were ruined. Their original assets that they had put on margin were gone or were worthless. The financial and banking interests that had extended the ostensibly unending lines of credit had no avenue of recourse or recovery and subsequently failed. Even the people who did not invest in the market saw their life savings on deposit evaporate before they could reach the bank. All aspects of American society were hit by the crash. It would take a world war to pull us out of the clutches of the depression. It would be some time before the stock market would return to its crucial role in the American economy, for which it was designed.

Where Margin Is Appropriate in Today's Market

In today's stock market, a tighter system of checks and balances has been instituted to prevent runaway market crashes, as in 1929. There are regulations on what type of securities can be margined, and there are limits on the percentage of outstanding debit balances. These safeguards were designed to protect the financial market system as a whole, not the individual investor. Regardless of the advances to control margin investing, the concept is still not appropriate for the masses.

Margin trading does have its place for a select few of the investing public. Those individuals with the asset diversity and the net worth of an institution qualify to benefit from using a credit line for investing. The qualified margin client must have very aggressive investment return aspirations and enough liquid capital for back up, just in case the portfolio takes a tumble. If a person can invest with margin and not be leveraged beyond her normal financial capacities, then the idea can make sense. But this investor would have to have the entire amount of the debit balance held in reserve elsewhere. This cash reserve would have to be earning a better return than what the leveraged investor is paying in fees and interest for her margin account. Otherwise, the cash reserve should be put in the stock account and the interest charges could be avoided.

This cash reserve must be available in case of margin call, and it must be performing well enough to offset the costs of leverage. This brings up an interesting question, especially when the high percentage of fees charged on margin accounts is considered. If the funds being held elsewhere in reserve are performing well enough to more than offset the inherent cost of leverage, why not move the assets in the margin account to where the reserve cash is held?

Additional Burdens for the Margined Investor

It is a simple task to determine who is not appropriate for a margin account. A mere glance at the clients with current margin accounts will reveal the majority are investing beyond their means. The individual investor does not derive the bulk of his livelihood off net returns from the market. The individual attempts to build a portfolio from spare portions of current assets and monthly income. The standard goal is to create a secondary asset base that will supplement annual and retirement standards of living. Steady or drastic losses cannot be frequent occurrences if investing is to be a success. There are enough disadvantages already facing the individual investor. Drastic market losses can often be sudden and unforeseen. But the steady losses can often be predicted and prevented. A margin account is an example of a predictable and preventable steady loss.

The margined investor exposes herself to magnified abuse possibilities. If the advice and the stock positions being offered by the firm are bad, the leveraged client will suffer a multiplied ill effect. Accounts on margin mean bigger trades for bigger commissions. The temptation and occurrence of churning will be more prevalent. Churning refers to a broker, operating with or without a client's permission, entering frequent buy or sell orders solely for the purpose of generating commissions.

Abuse of the margin account investor also comes in the form of mental anguish. Beyond the nightmare of tax filing considerations, she must face the looming question of how she is doing, compared to the ongoing ravages of the debit balance yoke. This anguish is intensified by the cloud of confusion that accompanies the margined portfolio.

This cloud is a valuable tool of less than ethical brokerage firms and brokers. It all starts with the monthly account statement. The statement for the margin account is difficult to read. The leveraged client must consider the current value of the securities that were margined, and the current value of the securities that were purchased on margin, and how they relate, percentagewise, with the ongoing debit balance.

Various figures are tallied and listed on the statement, including total account value, special miscellaneous account and the margin account's current buying power. None of these figures will tell the leveraged client whether she is up or down for the year. The margin account statement will also list the various charges of debit balance interest and transactional commissions. Somewhere within this monthly quagmire, the idea of determining the true, net return of the margin account is lost. The leveraged client should not feel bad for being confused, because the majority of stock brokers can't read a margin account statement either.

The broker doesn't need to completely understand margin accounts. All he has to do is take a glance at the account's current buying power, and he can see the client's current credit line. The broker doesn't worry about overbuying in the account, because somewhere, on the operations side of every firm, is a person who thoroughly understands the margin account concept. This person monitors the margin transactions of each trading day. The broker merely fills out the buy ticket and marks it "type 2," to signify a margin buy. If the purchase amount exceeds the margin account's current buying capacity, the ticket will be pulled by the monitoring operations personnel. This person will ensure the broker adjusts the purchase amount to fit within the account's current credit line. The firm wants to be sure it doesn't lend more money than there are securities that can be sold off to recover the loan. That kind of risk should only be endured by the clients.

The Hollow Promise from the Proponents of Margin

There will be multitudes of clients who cannot resist the call to margin account investing. There will be many people who read this and say that I am wrong. But a close examination of this group will show they are people who make their living from margined investors. Those individuals who have already experienced the wonderful world of leverage can identify with the points presented. Eventually these battered and beleaguered investors will realize the peril of their situation. They will free themselves from the shackles of their own credit line. For those who still feel they must go through the experience, I offer the following as a last ditch effort to talk them out of it.

Margin account investing is filled with smoke and promise. Proponents present the concept by skillfully exploiting the emotions of fear and greed. The ideals of achieving a higher level of investment sophistication, and the ability to take bigger advantage of pending market momentum, serve as additional endorsements of leveraged buying. With so much emphasis on the upside potential, the steady losses, in the form of fees and charges, and the multiplied downside possibilities, are not given equal billing. Motivated by the prospects of higher investment aspirations, a naive client will accept the pitch and boldly open a margin account.

Regardless of the objective, the margin account holds more promise for defeat than victory. If the leveraged portfolio's goal is to attain aggressive capital growth, then the hazards become magnified. The mixture of putting your portfolio on margin to participate in a brokerage firm's biased, block trade share purchase, and having to pay interest on and pay off a relatively substantial debit balance, while carrying the risk of margin calls, can prove lethal to your net asset value.

The use of margin can be disastrous for even the conservative investor. With the objective of safe and steady income, the best probable outcome would be for the positive and negative interest in the account to offset each other. The interest yield on a bond position, or the dividend yield from a stock, will rarely surpass the related debit interest charges and commissions. A run up in interest rates, or bad news concerning a bond issuer, can bring an income oriented portfolio's value down drastically. The drop can require the liquidation of positions. The client will still be enslaved to an outstanding debit balance. Market downturns that force margined investors to sell their original securities occur equally with aggressively and conservatively leveraged endeavors.

The individual investor is not a deep-pocketed cash cow who can sustain major stock market set backs. He is not a huge corporate or municipal entity that can expect the federal government to institute a tax payer bail out, if the portfolio should crash. The individual investor is the sacrificial lamb of choice, by the rest of the market players. The advice that reaches the investor is tainted with bias and ulterior motive. To the lone client, the only way margin account investing can be beneficial is with a prolonged streak of double or triple price runs on stock positions. The only ways this could be achieved are by having an exclusive inside track of information or by being blessed with incredible luck.

The Margined Investor Becomes an Institutional Tool

Margin account investing is a sucker's game. The disadvantages of interest charges and an outstanding debit balance go to the individual. The risk of stock purchases, in amounts beyond one's normal fiscal means, and the risk of having to sell original positions to satisfy a margin call, are also carried by the individual.

To the firm go all the benefits of margin investing. For the firm, it's risk-free. Its credit line is completely secured by the leveraged client's assets. The firm will make a bit more commission, if it has to sell a client's stock to retrieve the debit balance. A firm can wield more buying power from an investor on margin. Increased buying power can be focused into the stocks that the firm needs to move, often right out of its own inventory. This increased buying power is accompanied by larger transaction fees, higher account activity and a bigger market muscle to show to prospective institutional and investment banking clients. Perhaps a certain number of individual investors do have to enter the margin arena to keep the stock market world turning. But it's up to the individual to decide if she is to be part of that group.

For individual investors, the margin account is a modern-day Siren, coaxing their portfolios to a jagged reef of inherent, yet preventable losses. If you choose to answer the call and embrace the idea of leveraged investing, you will discover the 13th and 14th ways you lose money.

WAY #13: *Change your cash account to a margin account.* In an instant, you'll be able to magnify your financial involvement in the wonderful opportunities being presented by your altruistic investment firm. Don't worry about adding any capital; now you're a valued client with a credit line. If the market turns sour, your margin commitment will be satisfied by the firm selling what remains of your portfolio. It's just one more thing that you won't have to worry about.

WAY #14: *Don't trouble yourself with calculating the interest charges from your margin debit compared with the return of your leveraged portfolio.* Especially if your objective is income. You just might spoil the pleasant surprise at the end of the year, when you realize the accumulated interest charges negated any positive yield. At least you won't have to worry about taxable income. Unless, of course, your state doesn't allow deductions for margin interest charges and makes you pay taxes on the negated income anyway.

CHAPTER 9

Options Abuse: Inevitable Losses Through Incorrect Use

The Ways You Lose: 15

A Tradition of Improper Use

Options are the misunderstood and misused derivative, contractual investment product. I've included the word *derivative* because an option's value depends on the movement of the particular stock from which it derives. I've also included the word *contract* in this description because an option's profit or loss depends on the related stock moving in the right direction within a certain period of time.

Only a small amount of capital is required to reap potential rewards of several times the original option investment. The results can be determined in less than 90 days. However, if one possessed the intestinal fortitude to author an option contract for sale to the public, a nice chunk of change could be had without much probable repercussions.

Confused, yet somehow intrigued by this unique opportunity? Well, you've got a lot of company. The bulk of straight option investors form one of the biggest chapters of the stock market suckers' club. Its existence is due mainly to the masses' efforts to push an investment product far beyond its intended limitations.

Most individual investors have heard of options. In every peer group or social setting, there exists one person, who feels compelled to share the tale of his new, sophisticated investment vehicle. The word is tossed around in the financial news media. The options sector of the stock market trades in tremendous daily volumes. The daily tabulations indicating the closing option prices occupy their own space in the paper's financial section. There is no proficiency rating required of individuals venturing into options investing, because the majority of those people who do place their funds in the options market possess no knowledge of this derivative product before, during or after their involvement.

The individual investor is initially attracted to options because of their legendary image. One imagines two sophisticated, tuxedo-clad theater patrons discussing their recently established option positions, during an intermission. Supporting such appealing scenarios are the vast array of awe inspiring option stories that circulate the lunchrooms and happy hours across this fine land. As if part of an ancient tribal heritage, these tales of market triumph are passed from one lay-person to another. The story line conveys incredible financial success by way of an options position. The actual person depicted is never quite clear. He is usually the cousin of someone's brother-in-law or a roommate from college. The important part is that this person had to merely put down a small amount of cash, and he was able to make several times that amount, within a few months. The establishment of the story's hard facts are not necessary to create curiosity within the listener. The attraction to options takes hold, and the attentive individual investor takes a motivated leap into further action.

A feeling of encouragement follows this initial attraction. The investor makes a phone call to the brokerage firm to inquire about options. She is glad to learn that many of the facts heard in the lunchroom were true. The investment professional confirms that a small amount of money can be put at risk to reap potentially high rewards within a matter of weeks. The investor feels a warm glow. This could be the long-awaited break that finally leads to investment success. She tells the broker to mail the material known as the options agreement. The investor's warm feeling is intensified when the broker informs her that she can buy some options today and mail back the required paperwork later.

This individual investor begins to experience feelings of amazement from her newly purchased options. She becomes intrigued by the drastic price fluctuations during a single market day. She knows her options will move, in a degree of coordination, with the related stock. She observes how each slight movement in the related stock price sends a similar, yet greater percentage of movement in the stock's option contract.

The daily peaks and valleys are quick, almost too quick to make a decision of selling over holding. Although these option price movements are in significant percentages, considering the small amount of money invested and the relatively lofty fees, the profit windows have yet to be open beyond the break-even point. However, the investor is still amazed with all this movement. She feels excited to be a part of something so active and substantial. The images of the intense, sophisticated market action of the big Wall Street players fills her mind. She is enveloped by this atmosphere of extreme fluctuation and exaggerated potential. All she can do is standby and listen to her heart rate and blood pressure elevate, while watching the ticker screen on the financial news report.

Then it all comes to an abrupt end. The witching hour is sounded. After a mental jaunt through the feelings of attraction, encouragement and amazement, the investor is left with the feeling of confusion. This occurs upon the expiration of the options contract. When the designated time period of this investment is complete, its privileges and obligations become void. This option will no longer trade and will no longer have a market value listed in the evening paper. Up to this point, if the investor has not sold or exercised the prerogative of the options contract, her investment will expire worthless. This is the typical result of the option experience for the investor.

If the above scenario appears unclear, and many of its points poorly defined, then you share the same understanding of most individual investors when they venture into the option contract world. A basic understanding of option contracts becomes a low priority for the over-anxious individuals entering this action-packed sector of high finance. The excitement acts like a magnet. The buy orders are placed, and the checks are mailed to cover the purchase. Then the new options owner sits back and lets it all happen to him. He doesn't understand his investment, but he hopes for the best from his uneducated guess. For these investors, it would have been best had they experienced a substantial loss the first time around. At least they would not continue to chase a pipe dream of investment success by misusing a derivative investment product.

Fundamental knowledge, specified objective, and a sound and disciplined investment strategy should become primary components of the investor's market philosophy. Yet thousands of individual investors continue to pour their money into investment products, without knowing the what or the why behind their decision. These poorly understood investments are held by their owners, who have no definite objective in mind. The individual option investor fits this profile. To even understand the aforementioned options scenario, much less commit one's investment funds, one must grasp the basics of this derivative investment product.

Options Defined

For the purist, there are only two types of market investments. There are stocks and there are bonds. The former is an equity and the latter is a debt instrument. Equities represent ownership and provide the potential of capital gain. Debt instruments represent money on loan to another entity and provide interest income. Options do not fall into either of these categories. Although not a packaged product like a mutual fund or an annuity, options also exist beyond the realm of the two pure forms of market investment.

The derivative sector is where options dwell. The fortunes and fate of a particular option depend on the movement of the publicly traded instrument from which it derives. Options can derive from such instruments as stocks, indexes or commodity futures.

The explanations in this chapter pertain to stock options. The stock from which a particular stock option derives provides the primary catalyst for movement in the market price of the option. The degree and direction taken by the underlying stock is immediately reflected in the price of the related option. As overwhelming buying or selling pressure moves the stock price, similar pressure affects the option. In terms of percentage price movement, it should be noted that slight fluctuations in the stock price usually cause magnified ripples in the option price.

Once the stock option is chosen, the option contract dictates the time period and the rights granted to its owner. The contract gives the holder the right to do something for a certain period of time. The exercise of this right is the option of the investor, hence the name. A great way to support or to protect a current market position is to buy a relevant option contract. This idea brings us to the original, intended use of options.

Proper Use of Options as Initially Designed

Stock options were initially introduced as a means of protecting a stock or a cash position. An investor can buy contractually binding support of her portfolio, for a certain period of time. Buying an option helps to temporarily temper the necessary risks of playing the market, for a nominal fee.

When holding a large position of one stock issue, the investor's biggest worry is the ever possible demise of that stock's market value. A sell-off can occur without warning, and it is anyone's guess if the pummeled share prices will ever recover. Should a shareholder begin to sense a major price drop is imminent, she has three choices of action.

She can ignore the sensations of possible pending disaster. Whether the feelings originate from an inexplicable internal source, or there is mounting evidence of approaching and massive selling pressure, the investor could fight the urges to take any action. She could stick with her stress-inducing stock position and continue to harbor all the anxiety. This is an unacceptable situation. She should not allow herself to be held hostage by her portfolio. All the mental strain resulting from the extenuating circumstances of this stock's immediate future has made her a psychological prisoner. An investment endeavor, much like a relationship or an occupation, is no longer worthwhile if it starts to decrease one's psychological quality of life.

So perhaps holding the stock position is not the best solution to her dilemma. The investor could simply sell the stock, regardless of the selling being for profit, loss or break-even. She could be rid of the stock and all the accompanying worry. However, the sell wouldn't provide complete mental freedom. It is possible she has grown emotionally attached to the stock, which is a very financially dangerous habit. This stock might be a great source of dividend income, or there is profit potential just beyond its questionable, immediate future. Most likely, her hesitance to sell is based on a high degree of uncertainty. She is not totally convinced of the credibility behind the original warning signals. She knows it is always possible the small internal voice or the outside suggestive evidence is wrong. The immediate fate and fortunes of her stock might just as well be on the verge of a powerful upward move. This could very well be the most inopportune moment to unload her shares. This thought is further proof of investment-driven psychological bondage.

The third possible course of action involves a compromise. This compromise does cost money, for the temporary mental relief it provides. If the investor is convinced that some disaster is going to befall her share price within the next 90 days, she can buy a relevant option contract. She will choose the type according to the anticipated direction of the share price and when she feels it will occur.

The investor owns 3,000 shares of HRSE. The current price for the Horse Corporation shares is $12. Sometime in the next 60 days, the investor has reason to believe, derogatory news pertaining to the Horse Corporation is going to be released. There could be severe ramifications to the share price. This belief of pending bad news is not powerful enough to drive the investor to sell her shares. A large dose of uncertainty exists on either side of this issue. She remedies her situation with the purchase of an option contract.

Her newly purchased option contract is good for 90 days. The exact expiration date of the contract is included in the symbol under which it trades. This symbol (e.g., HRSAB) will be very similar to that of the stock's symbol, from which it derives. The rights of the option owner can be found in the title of the contract. All the aspects of the option contract can be found in its symbol, but it is much easier to read in its long form.

In this case, the investor purchases the right to sell her stock at $10, at any time over the next 90 days. If her HRSE shares were to drop to $5 the next day or in 89 days, she owns the right to sell them for $10 a share. Her shares are trading at $12 for the moment. If the projected share price disaster never happens, then she purchased a secure piece of mind for 90 days. If the disaster becomes a reality, then her protective option purchase kept a small market setback from becoming a major monetary loss.

The Protective Aspects of Options

An option contract can also be used to protect a large cash position. There are times, in an uncertain market, when it is wise to hold assets in the form of cash. However, should certain sections of the market begin a sudden upward surge, those individuals sitting on the sidelines would miss out on all the fun and profit. An option purchase can grant the opportunity to participate in a rally, without having to commit a large portion of cash.

The investor feels the Horse Corporation is going to experience an excellent year, but he is uncertain of its immediate prospects over the next 90 days. HRSE shares have moved up to $15, from $12, over the last few weeks. The question is whether to buy the stock now for its longer-term potential, or to wait until the short-term uncertainty has passed. Instead of subjecting himself to the mental anguish of indecisiveness, he buys an option contract appropriate to his situation.

He now owns the right to buy HRSE at $17, at any time, over the next 90 days. If HRSE should rally to $25, he could exercise his option to buy the stock at $17. Regardless of what occurs before the expiration of the contract, the investor accomplishes two things. First, he ensures he can buy a stock at a lower price should it run up, even though he hasn't actually committed cash to the shares. Second, if the stock price does not move up or if it drops during the contract period, he avoids committing cash at a higher point.

The two investors portrayed above, one with a large stock position and the other with a large cash position, have used options properly. Options were designed to protect current portfolio positions. Options were also initially intended to support the investor's planning of market moves, without requiring him to actually commit large amounts of capital during times of uncertainty. The first option granted the right to sell a stock under certain conditions for a specified period of time. The second option granted the right to buy a stock under certain conditions for a specified period of time. These are two basic types of options.

The Two Distinctive Forms of Options: The Put Option and the Call Option

Option contracts come in two forms: calls and puts. A call grants the right to buy a stock under certain circumstances. A put grants the right to sell a stock under certain circumstances. An easy way to remember the difference is to consider the call as calling a stock to you, and to consider the put as putting a stock away to someone else. Option contracts can be purchased or an investor can sell them into the market. This is referred to as writing an option contract.

Let's say an investor is holding 1,000 shares of HRSE at $12, which he bought for $6 per share. He is pleased with the results so far and wants to stay in for more, but he is also concerned about any potential down-slide. He can protect his profits, and limit any possible losses, by purchasing ten put options. He can choose the price at which he can sell the stock and the time period he wants for this downside protection. The closer the put price is to the stock's current market price, and the longer the time period of the contract, the more expensive the option price will be. One option contract represents a right that can be exercised on 100 shares of stock.

In this case, the investor buys ten put options with a strike price of $10 that expire in 90 days. The strike price refers to the price at which the option can be exercised. These puts allow the investor to sell the stock at $10 during the contract period. If these put options have a current market price of ¾, then they are $75 each. The investor will pay $750 for this 90-day insurance policy on his stock position.

The investor also can choose to sell a put to the market, the same as writing a put. He is holding shares of HRSE at $12, which he bought for $6. However, this time he chooses a different path than before. He sells the stock and keeps the $12,000 of proceeds in cash reserve. The investor senses the HRSE stock has peaked for the moment. He has his principal and his profits off the table, and he decides to make a bit more money from HRSE while he maintains his cash position.

He sells the very ten put options that were purchased earlier. Remember, for every buyer in the market, there must be a seller. This time he is the seller, or writer, of those put options. He is now obligated to buy 1,000 shares of HRSE at $10 per share. This obligation has to be fulfilled, if the puts are exercised during the next 90 days. When the investor sells these puts, at a current market price of ¾, he will receive $75 for each one, or $750 total. If the stock drops and the puts are exercised, he has more than enough cash to fulfill the contract, and he is buying the shares for $2 less than he had originally sold them. If the stock stays flat or moves up, the puts will not be exercised and he makes $750, or a quick 6¼ percent on his $12,000 in 90 days. Upon expiration of the put contracts, he can consider selling more puts with the reserve cash backing him up.

The other form of an option contract is the call. The owner of a call option has the right to purchase a stock for a specified price and time. Returning to HRSE, the stock is currently trading at $10. The investor is maintaining a cash position and considering a purchase of 1,000 shares of HRSE. She is hesitant to commit her cash now, but doesn't want to miss out on a possible opportunity, either.

She decides buying call options is the most sensible middle ground. The investor buys ten calls with a strike price of $12 and an expiration in 180 days. The price of each contract is 1¼, for a total amount due of $1,250. She does not have to commit any more capital, yet maintains the right to buy 1,000 shares at $12, should the stock start an upward push over the next 180 days.

Over the next few weeks, there is a growing amount of buying interest in HRSE. The trading volume starts to increase and the share price begins to inch upward. Heavy promotion and some positive news releases cause the stock to jump several points. HRSE is now trading at $18, and the investor with the related call options is elated. She decides to exercise her calls and buys the 1,000 shares. However, as is her right, she pays only $12 for the currently higher priced stock. Pleased with her call option experience thus far, she decides to try it from the other side. To sell, or write, some call options to the market is her next move.

The big rally that pushed HRSE to $18 has subsided. It is anyone's guess if the stock will maintain its current position for the short term. The investor feels very optimistic about the Horse Corporation's fortunes over the next 12 months. However, she is uncertain about the next two business quarters. She would also like to create some short-term income from the position, while waiting for her projected long-term gains. She covers her bases by selling ten calls, with strike prices of $20, over the next 180 days. Her selling price is 1⅞, or $187.50 per contract. The total proceeds from the sell are $1,875.

There are a few different possibilities over the next 180 days. If HRSE does not move above $20, before the contract expires, then the investor will simply make $1,875 profit. In the event that HRSE does move above $20, it is possible the investor will have to fulfill the obligations of the calls she sold. If HRSE moves high enough to make up for the price of the calls and provide a decent profit margin, the owner of the calls might elect to exercise his rights. In this case the investor is obligated to sell her 1,000 shares of HRSE to the call owner at $20. Either way, the investor has had a decent 180-day market experience. She is already sitting on a nice stock profit, because of the exercise of her previous call option purchase. When she sold the ten calls into the market she made over 10 percent in six months on her 1,000 shares at $18. She actually made over 15 percent, if you remember she only had to pay $12 per share.

She does even better if the calls she sold are exercised, because that means she is obligated to sell her shares at $20, which is a $2 profit per share. This would add a $2,000 capital gain to $1,875 in call sale proceeds, for a return of 22 percent in less than 180 days. This return is much higher if you again remember this investor's original purchase price for the stock was $12 per share.

The Essential Underlying Principles for the Proper Use of Options

The previous examples demonstrate proper uses of option contracts. They are best used in support of current positions. The decision to buy a call or a put should be based on personal predictions of the related security's pending direction. Option investments are supposed to be protective measures, to prevent an investor from losing profit or principal. Options can prevent an investor from missing a market opportunity, due to hesitance to commit a large amount of capital. There are times when the prudent decision is to sell or write call and put options into the market. This decision should have a dual objective: To profit from the proceeds and to support an investment strategy or to protect a current position, whether it is a stock or cash reserves.

Always remember, an option is a time sensitive investment. Whether the contract period is 90 days or two years, the option's life span is predetermined. The option's market value, rights and obligations do not progress beyond its expiration date. The buyers and sellers on either side of an option's transaction are both betting their predictions are right and the other side's are wrong. Both sides know it will all be decided before the arrival of the witching hour. This rings in the moment the option contract becomes null and void.

The current market price for any option will depend on a few variables. The amount of time left before the expiration date, and the distance between the strike price and the current market price of the related stock, will both have an influence on the option price. If a call has a strike price of $10 and the related stock is currently trading at $11, then it is considered to be in the money. This would justify a much higher purchase price because it is currently a fairly safe bet. Of course, a temporary state of imbalance between the buying and selling interest, on either side of an option's market, will have the biggest short-term influence of the contract price. This imbalance is in direct relation to the current status of the related stock.

Any movement in the related stock will have a magnified effect on its options. A typical example would be a $25 stock, making a 10 percent move, could cause its call options to move over 50 percent. There is no set ratio formula between the price movement of the option contracts and the related stocks. Just keep in mind, slight movement in the related stock will result in a multiplied movement in the option, in terms of percentage change. The direction of the stock's movement dictates how the calls or the puts are affected.

An option contract is much cheaper than 100 shares of the related stock. The price of these options move in greater percentages than that of the related stock. An option buy, over a buy of the related 100 shares of stock, gives a leveraged return potential and only a fraction of the cash is required. A $1,000 investment can be all that is required to play the market off the fortunes of $20,000 worth of stock. These ideals represent the origins of option contract misuse by the investing public.

An Account of the Typical Misuse of Options

Consider the following example of option misuse: An investor sees HRSE trading at $20 per share. He has a strong feeling that the Horse Corporation stock is about to make a substantial upward move. The investor does not want to commit the $20,000 to pick up 1,000 shares, but he does have the money to buy 10 call options, which represent 1,000 shares of HRSE. He purchases the calls, with a strike price of $24, which expire in 90 days. The calls are $100 each, for a total commitment of $1,000 based on the movement of $20,000 worth of stock. In theory, these calls grant the investor the right to buy HRSE at $24, no matter how high the price runs up in the next 90 days. He will be required to come up with $20,000, if he wants to exercise the rights of his options. But to buy the stock at a lower price is not his objective.

The investor's objective is to realize a capital gain solely from the call options. The attractive option stories, overheard at the gym and the office lunchroom, have convinced him of the wisdom behind this move. He is encouraged by the simplicity of the transaction. He merely requests the options agreement, enters the order with his broker and conducts a nightly vigil staring at his paper's financial section. As he watches his own options, he is amazed by some of the drastic moves of other contracts in the paper's listings. With confidence, he assures himself he is in the right type of investment.

This time the fortune fairies smile upon the investor. His window of opportunity arrives at the six-week mark. Up to that point, HRSE fluctuated only slightly from the share price of $20. The highest point of his call's bid price had been 1⅛, which is $112.50 per contract. There was a 12.5 percent profit showing in the position, but this investor, new to the high speed world of options, was hunting for elephant-sized capital gains.

After six weeks of holding the options, a flurry of buying activity envelops the HRSE shares. The stock moves up to 22⅛ in three days of trading, up almost 11 percent. The calls are up over 50 percent, to 1⁹⁄₁₆ (For option pricing, multiply the listed figure by 100). Each call is now worth $156.25. The total gross profit margin is $562.50. Considering this to be the most successful six weeks of his investment career, he sells his calls and takes the profit.

He spends the next day floating on air and beaming with pride. Option investing now holds a special place in his heart. The most he could have lost was the $1,000 for the ten calls. In six weeks, his gross profit was over 50 percent. Had he bought the 1,000 shares of HRSE, he would have had to come up with $20,000 and perhaps wait forever to make 50 percent on $20 shares. No, he is convinced, that kind of investing is for saps. Buying option contracts, solely for the inherent profit potential, is definitely the way to go.

Well, the best thing didn't happen to this investor. He didn't lose his entire investment the first time around. Initial success in the misuse of options often propels people down the road to ruin. The fees to buy and sell options are extremely high, in relative percentage to the amount of principal being invested. Even a successful option endeavor must have an exaggerated profit window to provide a reasonable amount of net proceeds.

Early triumphs from option misuse can lull the investor into a false sense of reality. He will forget the finite lifespan of his option's market value. He will forget two out of the three possibilities work against him, if he is a buyer of options. By following the strategy of misusing options, he could win 14 times in a row and on the 15th lose more than the total previous wins. The ultimate financial punishment will come to the investor, if his early option success creates a confidence of the most dangerous level. He discovers the way to receive immediate proceeds by selling, or writing, option contracts to the market. At this point, the original leverage is now working against him.

With the fundamental knowledge of options under your belt, let's continue to follow the previous investor's trail. It is a typical story of an individual investor being lured into misusing options, even though the odds of overall success are stacked heavily against him.

The Disadvantageous Position of the Options Abuser

The enticement, the approval, and the early success of the option experience is now behind the investor. He boldly charges further into the depths of his new-found investment arena. In relation to his personal net worth, the investor is ready to sink some real money into options. His perceptions of reality have already been tainted by the speed and size of the gross profit margin from his initial derivative endeavor. The true picture of risk and related fees is not in focus. In his haste and ignorance, he fails to see the disadvantages stacked against him.

The first disadvantage is the high relative cost of buying options. In the investor's initial purchase of calls, he buys ten contracts at $100 each, plus commission. The total amount of principal was $1,000. Depending on what firm he dealt with, the minimum commission charged would range between $60 and $100. In this case, we'll split the difference and work with the commission charge of $80. Thus, upon buying the calls, he paid the current spread plus the 8 percent commission.

When he sold his call position, the total market value was $1,562.50. This amount of principal was still within the minimum commission range. Another $80 was charged on the sell. After the related fees, but before taxes, the investor still made a quick 40 percent. He was fortunate the gross profit margin was wide enough to absorb the high percentage cost of option investing. Many brokerage houses have limits on the commission percentages charged on stock or bond purchases. If the amount of principal being invested is so low it puts the house's minimum commission charge above 5 percent, the trade will often be declined. However, it is very rare to find this rule being enforced on option business. The great number of individual investors who routinely put less than $1,800 into their option transactions repeatedly subject themselves to excessive commissions.

The second disadvantage of buying an option is the finite time factor. Included in the option's symbol is the expiration date. Beyond this date the contract becomes null and void. The day of expiration is the last day the contract will trade or hold any market value. Time is working against the option buyer. Every day his call contract moves a little closer to becoming completely worthless. In relation to the investor's initial options experience, he missed the finality of the expiration date and got away with option contract misuse. He purchased the calls solely for the profit potential in the contracts themselves. He did not establish the call position in support of other current assets or an overall strategy. Had the related stock not moved during the 90 days of the call contracts' life, the profit window would have never appeared. The calls would have expired, worthless, and the investor would have lost the entire $1,000. However, the initial loss didn't happen, and now he's hooked for bigger money.

The third disadvantage facing the misguided option buyer pertains to the odds of success. During a contract period, the related stock price can take three possible directions. The related stock price's movement is the primary catalyst to drive the option price. The related stock price can move up, down or sideways (remain flat). Depending on whether the investor purchased a call or a put, only one of these possibilities would work in his favor. Sideways movement would be bad for either type of option. Upward movement favors the owner of a call. Downward movement favors the owner of a put. The right direction of movement would have to occur within the contract period and provide enough profit margin to offset the high percentage of related fees.

In the case of the investor's initial option endeavor, the related stock did move in the right direction. It moved enough to provide an adequate profit margin, and the move occurred before the contract's expiration date. With all the possible ways the option investor could lose his entire investment, the triple combination, essential to option success, should be considered the long shot.

After Early Success, the Options Abuser Runs Headlong Towards Disaster

Nevertheless, the investor is undaunted by his disadvantageous position, which he does not see anyway. He boldly telephones his broker. One good option play warrants another. This is the type of call for which brokers live, because the subject matter pertains to a transaction. It is the amount of transactions, in any given month, that determines a broker's value as a human being. Option trades can be a nice addition to a broker's monthly production total. If enough individuals, with only about $500 to invest, can be gathered and put into options, the minimum commission charges can really add up. There is also a good chance that many of these option positions will generate minimum sell commissions in the very near future.

Options, as a windfall source of commissions, can also become a nightmare for the broker. There are many brokers who will not do an option transaction, unless it is being entered for the proper reasons. If the client wants to misuse options, the business will often be declined because the commission isn't worth all the potential trouble.

The large number of individuals who improperly invest in options do so with a dollar amount that warrants the minimum commission charge. Since these option investors are only interested in trying to sell the contract at a profit before the expiration date, they are going to watch how the contract trades very closely. This means the broker can expect many phone calls from these clients wanting an option quote and advice. The mental load of counseling these jittery, junior investors can make the broker's percentage of that minimum commission appear mighty thin. A stockbroker knows the best clients are the ones who are only heard from when their deposit check hits the account.

We can assume the investor's broker accepts the next option buy order. The investor came away with about $1,500 from his initial option play. He decides to add another $1,000 and purchase $2,500 worth of call contracts. He will probably continue to invest in this pattern, if he is again blessed with the essential triple combination: movement in the right direction, with a sufficient amount of profit margin and within the right period of time. However, the market will eventually turn against him. The related stock won't respond in a favorable way, and he won't have the luxury of being able to wait out the correction. The option expiration date will arrive and render his position worthless. Regardless of how many consecutive victories he enjoyed, the inevitable and periodic option loss can wipe out the previous successes.

Things can be worse. Improperly investing in options can lead to a greater loss than the mere initial amount of principal. An early string of victories can build a sense of false confidence. It can be so strong, the uneducated investor develops the bravado to go beyond merely buying options for the wrong reasons. This investor recklessly heeds the yearning to sell options to the market. Just as he improperly bought options, he conducts his selling, or writing, of the contracts in the same fashion. The calls and puts that he offers to the market are uncovered, also referred to as naked. He sells these merely for the immediate proceeds, not to protect current assets or in support of a larger investment strategy. This kind of short-sighted option selling places the investor in a self-imposed, precarious position.

Naked option selling has been the financial Waterloo for many overzealous and falsely confident investors. The option investor now decides to sell ten call contracts into the market. The related stock is HRSE, and the shares are currently trading at $20. The investor feels fairly certain there will not be a substantial move up in Horse Corporation stock, for at least three months. The current market price for HRSE calls, with strike price of $22 and 90 days until the expiration date, is $150 per contract. He sells ten of the calls for a quick $1,500 in proceeds. The buyer of these calls now owns the right, for the next 90 days, to purchase 1,000 shares of HRSE for $22 from the investor. HRSE would have to go to at least $24 before the owner of the calls would be motivated to exercise the right of his options. The $1,500 the owner paid for the calls adds another $1.50 to the break-even price per share. In this case, the break even price per share is $23.50.

The call seller is operating on the weak end of a proper risk-reward ratio. The seller is committed to an uncovered call obligation. He does not currently own 1,000 shares of HRSE, which is what he would have to come up with if the ten calls are exercised. He is risking the requirement to buy at least $24,000 worth of stock in the market, just to make $1,500 in option sale proceeds. This strategy is obviously not sound, yet it is implemented by members of the investing public every market day.

This potentially self-destructive investment approach is the same if an investor is selling puts, yet had no real interest in the related stock. He just sold the puts for the immediate proceeds. The stock was at $22 and the puts had a strike price of $20. If the stock price starts to drop, the seller might have to spend $20,000 for a stock he didn't want, just to make $1,500 in proceeds. Selling uncovered options is a display of poor judgment and a poor benefit cost analysis.

The First Step to Recovery from Options Abuse Is Acknowledgment

There is a proper way to conduct option investing. Under the correct circumstances, the option market can provide excellent protection for current assets and sound support for larger investment strategies. But the misuse of these derivative products is widespread. Whether the investing public is improperly buying or selling option contracts, the pitfalls are similar. Time, the odds, and the high transactional and potential costs, are all working against the uninformed individual investor. How you invest in options is a premarket decision that can be the 15th way you lose money.

WAY #15: *For quick capital gains with easy terms, consider the purchase of option contracts to have the ultimate risk-reward ratio.* Within the brief contract period, a minimal amount invested can potentially multiply several times. The option market offers the individual investor the leverage to play off the movement of large positions, without actually having the capital or sound reason. For those individuals seeking immediate income, naked or uncovered option selling proves to the world that you've got the guts to push this derivative investment product well beyond its proper and intended use.

CHAPTER 10

The Realities of Mutual Funds

The Ways You Lose: 16, 17 and 18

A Cross-Examination of America's Most Popular Investment Product

The arena of mutual funds is a very popular place to lose money. Although this type of investment product can maintain decent unit price stability, substantial losses can accumulate in the various forms of fees.

A mutual fund is a packaged product. It is neither a pure stock nor bond instrument. A mutual fund is designed to simulate the performance of a stock or a bond, or a combination of both. The vastness of this sector surpasses all other investment categories. The land mines that an investor can encounter are numerous. The majority of pitfalls are not caused by the crooks and the con men of the industry. It is the individuals who bring most of the monetary hardships on themselves. The primary causes originate from the myths harbored by the typical mutual fund investor.

Before proceeding further, let me offer the following disclaimer: A good mutual fund can be a good thing. Many funds have proven themselves to be excellent performers over the years. In concept, mutual funds can offer you the ability to participate in small increments, enjoy the security of asset allocation over a number of positions and receive the benefits of professional management. However, the sector also offers more opportunities to lose personal asset value than ever before. Few of the masses involved truly understand the vehicle into which they have placed their money.

The greatest myth, perpetuated by the self-sabotaging mutual fund investor, pertains to the concept of load. To believe in the existence of a true no-load fund is to believe in the existence of financial institutions that forgo profits in exchange for humanitarian service to the community.

There was many a day when a client would sit in front of my desk and extol the virtues of a certain mutual fund that charged nothing for the privilege of participation. What an incredible display of altruism. Apparently, the benevolent no-load mutual fund managers provide the common clay of the investment earth, with a free opportunity. I soon stopped trying to educate my clients on this topic. Most investors would be insulted at my attempts to reveal the true costs behind a "no-load." A stock broker quickly learns the advantages of telling clients what they want to hear, rather than what they need to hear.

The next great myth, by which retail venture capitalists shoot themselves in the foot, is perpetuated by a fund's promotional material. During the decision-making process, the individual investor searches for a fund that has previously posted solid returns and has earned high ratings. Organizations, such as Morningstar and Lipper, monitor the performance and activity of thousands of mutual funds. They assign ratings and hierarchic rankings in a multitude of categories. For virtually every possible combination of time-frame, market sector and investment objective, there will be a fund ranking and rating hierarchy.

However, the ranking and rating hierarchy is based on percentage returns within a specific period and area observed. The masses incorrectly believe these indicators of past results to be the best reference for choosing a particular fund. Even the most conventional market wisdom says past results cannot be a guarantee of future performance. The consideration of a fund's timeliness of investment focus or how it is managed and administered are ignored, because of the overwhelmingly perceived importance of a fund's historical chart. The historical rankings and ratings are made readily available by every fund's promotional literature, boldly displayed on an illuminated graph, in a glossy mailer. Its reviews, from either of the two monitoring organizations, are proudly quoted. Although these two organizations cover thousands of mutual funds, I have yet to see a fund's literature not represent itself as a top-ranked, stellar performer. Every fund's marketing department must master the art of self-serving interpretation.

There is a different reality behind those lofty performance numbers, self-touted by the mutual fund companies. It seems odd that every mutual fund can have the top rating and have been the number one performer in its sector. Well, actually, it is not that odd if one examines why. Morningstar and Lipper monitor, rate and rank mutual funds in every conceivable time period and category. A mutual fund company needs to determine when and in what aspect they were ever among the best. It could be during a week's time, two years ago, that they had the best interest yield for a whole seven days. Now they qualify to call themselves a top-rated, highly ranked performer.

The third myth is conceptual. It leads to a false sense of security. At some point in our nation's market history, it became ingrained in the minds of investors that mutual funds were the premier method of conservative investment. The appeal of establishing a position in a fund and making monthly contributions of discretionary income is widespread throughout the masses. The onslaught of well-aimed marketing has worked. The ideal has been created, and accepted, that mutual funds are the thing to buy, until one has built up the assets to construct a real portfolio. Individual investors keep a high degree of faith in this particular packaged product. They believe their fund management will provide a comfortable investment environment, which will ensure the increase of their asset value. The mutual fund is to be the cornerstone of their financial empire. With the confidence of zealots, the masses pour millions of dollars into the mutual fund sector each month.

These three great myths of mutual fund investing usually result in a bland, if not a negative, experience for most of those involved. The lessons learned show the asset losses can be as drastic as with any other investment. Granted, the pace of unit value losses is usually much slower than that of individual stocks. The pace of mutual fund unit value movement, in any direction, is often slow enough to lull even the problem coffee drinker to sleep.

At year-end statement time, the writing is on the wall for the individual investor. The conservative, steady and upward march in asset value has not materialized. The investor is left wondering why this once proud endeavor has not become the grand foundation of her personal financial fortress. The price for participation turned out to be much higher than originally thought. Fees and charges accumulated from overt and covert sources. The fund's lofty performance history did not have the decency to repeat itself, during the investor's particular time period of involvement. The frustrated search for answers begins. In desperation, the ideals of the three great myths are consulted. But no consolation is to be found in those false notions. An explanation can only come from scrutinizing the reality of it all.

The Inherent Costs of Mutual Fund Investment

So few of the faithful who cliff dive into the frothy sea of mutual funds ever take a detailed look into what they are plunging. An examination of this packaged product's blueprint can dispel the myths that blur prudent judgment. The costs to participate in a mutual fund come from a variety of different angles. Spread, load, management fees and service charges are the profit tools of the mutual fund companies. It is not in the fund's best interest for its investors to experience substantial gains or losses. Big gains or big losses might induce investor selling. The longer the fund holds an investor's money, the more revenue that can be reaped by the various profit tools. The fund's aim is to provide a comfortable, steady environment, to foster a long and lucrative relationship with its customers' money.

The Cost of the Mutual Fund Spread

Mutual fund companies use actual spreads and averaged spreads to quote the fund's unit prices. An actual spread will quote a bid and ask price. This spread is based on the bid and ask prices of the securities within the fund, plus any self-serving bias of the mutual fund's management.

If a mutual fund company quotes one price at which units can be bought or sold, the quote contains an averaged spread. The actual spread is calculated and then averaged for a single transaction price. To the novice investor, it might appear that the mutual fund company is foregoing the profit source of spreads. This perceived altruism is purely cosmetic. For whatever strategic marketing reason that the fund's management forgoes one profit tool, it certainly makes up the revenue by increasing the margin of its other profit tools. The marketing department knows that an investor who does not know how a fund makes its money rarely checks the true and total costs of the investment product.

The Various Types of Load Structure

The fund's particular load structure is the most recognized, yet misunderstood, form of participation fee. The terms *front-end load, back-end load* and *no-load* have become familiar vernacular. The first step on the road to recovery for those suffering from chronic self sabotage is to grasp an understanding of these three terms regarding loads.

A mutual fund with a front-end load is the most basic. This type is referred to as an "A" share or unit. If an investor puts in $10,000 and the load is 4.5 percent, then $450 is taken from the principal as the load charge. When the investor decides to sell his fund units, there is no charge for liquidation, regardless of the unit's market value at the time of the sale.

The mutual funds that charge a back-end load are a little more complicated. These are known as "B" shares. When $10,000 is placed into these types of units, no percentage of principal is taken out. Normally, the fund agrees not to make a load deduction, if the investor does not liquidate his units for at least a five-to-seven-year period. If a sell order is entered within the first two years of participation, then a higher load than the "A" share percentage is charged. This liquidation fee decreases in percentage of current market value as the five-to-seven-year period draws to completion.

From this comparison of "A" and "B" shares, the long-term mutual fund investor might immediately decide the latter is best. However, there are other factors to be considered. The "A" shares can offer better value per unit from the start because of a tighter spread.

When an investor purchases mutual fund units, he pays the ask price. The next day, he could sell his units for the lower bid price. If the spread on the "A" share quote is $12.22 by $12.50, the spread on the comparable "B" share quote would be approximately $11.98 by $12.72. Thus, the "B" shares cost more per unit for less market value, the next day forward. Although the "B" shareholder is not charged an up-front load, this disadvantageous spread could be maintained for the entire period of holding the fund units. Additionally, there can be differences in the annual percentage of management fees charged for the two types of shares. The "B" shares will often cost slightly higher in this area. If you think about it, it should make perfect sense. When you buy a back-end load fund, the firm, the broker and the fund itself will all demand some sort of immediate payment. Without an up-front load, the money must come from somewhere.

Now we come to America's favorite: The no-load mutual fund. It is the great pipe dream of those who want something for nothing. Let me be perfectly clear. There is no such thing as a true, no-cost mutual fund. If someone thinks they are really getting something for free, then either they were one of my clients, or I really wish I would have gotten a hold of them during my broker days.

Please remember, a mutual fund is a packaged product. It is also actively managed and administered. All this costs money, and a mutual fund company is an entity with the objective to create profits. The mere privilege of handling your money just won't be enough. I have yet to find a charitable organization which extends complimentary fund management services. So how are these ostensibly "free" mutual funds possible? It's all very simple. The funds usually make it up in higher annual management fees. If they also maintain a wider spread, they'll make even more when unit holders buy and sell. Management always reserves the right to charge for basic services, such as a fee per call to the information line. No-load funds are often referred to as "C" shares. Your broker will be glad to put them in your account, even though you're apparently making him work for "free."

Open-Ended Funds versus Closed-Ended Funds

Regardless of the load arrangements, mutual funds come in two different forms: either open-ended or closed-ended. The individual investor needs to be aware of the disadvantages of both. Each type offers its own unique opportunity for you to lose money. Most investors do not know the difference between the two or which type they are holding.

The closed-end type of mutual fund carries its own stated objective, which could be anything from providing tax-free income to aggressive growth potential. Its total amount of units outstanding is limited to the original amount available during its initial offering period. After the offering period, it is listed on a major exchange and trades daily under its assigned symbol. Closed-end funds are professionally managed, and there is a relatively low annual fee charged for this service. Their performance is fairly easy to monitor, because the day's results are listed in the paper, just like an exchange-traded, individual stock issue. They don't seem like a bad deal, but the primary danger of closed-end mutual funds is in the method and timing of how they are presented to the investing public.

The national investment firms and mutual fund companies have become mass manufacturers of closed-end funds. Every month, there are a dozen new funds conducting initial offerings. In a period of about 60 days, enough money needs to be raised to list the fund's units on its chosen exchange. The new closed-end fund is normally offered in increments of $15 per unit. The operating mode of the institution bringing out the fund is the same as with any other initial public offering of a stock. No commission is charged to buy the IPO, but a commission is charged when the client wants to sell it. The brokers hit the phones to pitch the firm's new recommendation. The new fund's name, objective and unit price are included in the presentation. The broker's big close is to mention his firm is part of the offering group, so there will be no commission charged on the purchase-another fine opportunity for "free" investing.

It turns out to be not so free after all. The group of investment professionals involved demands payment for its valuable services. For every unit the investor buys at the offering price of $15 dollars, he usually receives about $13.80 in asset value. The cash difference between the offering price and the net asset value is used to pay the underwriting firms and the brokers. The broker payout is higher than that of a market purchase commission, after the offering.

I have yet to see a newly listed closed-end mutual fund not slip down in price, to reflect its true net asset value, within its first ten months of trading. This predictable drop in unit price occurs, regardless of how it eventually performs down the road. If providing income is within the particular closed-end fund's objective, the fact that no dividends are paid in the first 90 days of inception is rarely realized by the retail investor.

Remember the guidelines for an IPO: If a broker can get a typical client as much as he wants of an initial public offering, it's not worth owning at that price. If an investment is offered at no commission charge, then you know that you'll pay the price somewhere. That price is usually reflected in a decreased unit value about six months down the road. The broker is driven to only present this investment idea during the offering period. Why should a broker recommend the purchase of a previously issued closed-end fund at a standard commission, when his firm will give him greater rewards to push the merits of its next, new offering? By pushing the next closed-end fund offering, the broker can serve the whims of his institution, make a little more money for himself and satisfy the growing and uneducated desire of the investing public for no-load or free investing.

Open-Ended Mutual Funds

The other form of mutual fund investing is of the open-end variety. They are available in all the different objective packages of their closed-end brethren. Although closed-end funds charge stock-type commissions for buy and sell orders, open-end funds can be bought and sold under any of the three load structures. Open-end funds usually have higher annual management fees. There is no limit on the amount of units available for any particular open-end fund. A simple phone call to the company, or your broker, and you can buy more. They are not traded on an exchange, and their buy and sell market is maintained by the mutual fund company. Herein lies the danger of open-end mutual funds.

The assets within a mutual fund are allocated among a certain portfolio of securities. The current market value of those securities, divided by the amount of units outstanding, should be a rough indicator of the current unit price. However, since the open-end mutual fund company controls its own market, it leaves a lot of room for biased, self-serving adjustments on the bid and ask prices. The power of supply and demand is still a governing force on open-end fund unit prices. The advantages go to the fund company. During spurts of buying strength, the fund can move up the asking price for units, beyond what the temporary demand would normally justify. It is their option to bring the bid, or liquidation price, up accordingly during this time.

This is the beauty of the adjustable spread. When selling pressure is anticipated, the fund can simply drop the price at which units could be sold, until the liquidation push is over. With so many units outstanding, just a slight percentage adjustment in the spread can mean a quick windfall of profits.

The open-end fund investor will be held at the biggest disadvantage at the time of a market crash. Granted, times like these hit everybody and every sector hard, but not for such a prolonged period of time. An example would be the crash of October 1987. As the indexes started to slide, the selling momentum began to roll. Among the most panicked group were the conservative mutual fund investors. For over 30 days, the phone lines of the mutual fund companies were jammed with sell orders. The liquidation prices were adjusted down accordingly. The investors who could not get through by phone during this period did the best. By the spring most of the indexes were back up, and those who sold were buying back again at higher prices. It was a great time to own an open-end mutual fund company.

The Dangers of Mutual Fund Proliferation

In our quest to see the reality of it all concerning mutual funds, we must observe another ominous fact of the relative dilution of the product sector. There are more mutual funds available for purchase than there are stocks being publicly traded. This proliferation has created a "dime a dozen status." Remember that for any security to go up in price, more buying power has to go in after you than was there before you. Even a mammoth bull buying run would be severely diluted, because the purchase frenzy would be spread so thin among all the funds. Each one of the thousands of funds is managed by someone who is supposed to be infinitely qualified. The area of fund managers has definitely become a stretched talent pool. Expect each competent fund manager to be flanked by a great number of lesser talents.

Regarding accessibility and accountability of a fund's management, the mutual fund investor will never speak directly with their mutual fund manager. There will never be a personal or phone consultation to discuss strategy or market philosophy. Of course with the size of most funds, that would not be practical or possible. There isn't even the opportunity to consider the pending transactions, before they are executed by the manager. Any accountability is provided well after the fact. This is usually in the form of an incomprehensible quarterly statement.

Basically, the investor sends a check to the fund and just hopes for the best. Complete discretion is granted to a distant and unknown fund manager, in return for a package of fund materials, touting the manager as the greatest and most qualified person in the world. Retail brokers dream of being able to operate in this kind of situation. If they could move their clients' money around at will, without having to talk to them before or after, and not have to worry about complaints or arbitration for churning or unauthorized trades, it would be a dream come true. Most clients would eventually put an end to this situation if it was being done by their broker. But disguise it in the form of a mutual fund and it suddenly appears to be acceptable.

The individual investor should be armed with the following absolute truth: The same mutual fund that is being recommended to you by your firm's broker is definitely not in his own account. This absolute truth is also applicable to most investment recommendations, unless the broker is trying to sell you the recommendation directly from his firm's inventory. The institutions operating in the financial markets do not share in the public's pursuit of mutual fund investment. Ever wonder why a mutual fund company doesn't choose to own mutual funds in its portfolio? Perhaps those who truly understand, hold a different view of these packaged investment products.

Actions of Those Who Understand Mutual Funds and Those Who Don't

There is a traditional difference in the market institutions' approach to mutual funds, than the individual investors' approach. This difference is based in the institutions' understanding of mutual fund structure and the lack of understanding by individual investors.

For the market institution, it is quite simple: Never buy another market institution's packaged product, but always help your clients with their purchase of such products and reap the rewards of immediate commissions and incentive payouts from the grateful mutual fund company. Better yet, the savvy market institution forms its own mutual fund to sell to the investing public. An 800 number, a professional looking prospectus, a catchy fund name and an overallocated portfolio are all that is needed to become a mutual fund company. The womblike investment atmosphere is an irresistible magnet to the wallets and checkbooks of individuals everywhere.

The profit margin available to mutual fund companies is the prime reason for the existence of more mutual funds than there are publicly traded stocks. The business is just too good, and the product is too eagerly accepted by the investing public, for most market institutions to pass up offering their own mutual fund. A fund's success depends on an abundant key ingredient: The investment habits of the typical mutual fund investor.

My friend, Charlie, is the epitome of the classic mutual fund investor. The discipline and principles that he uses to guide his life do not apply to his investment endeavors. Charlie is an F-18 pilot in the United States Marine Corps. His expertise and his accomplishments have placed him at the top of the military aviation community. The other aspects of his life also reflect a history of superior achievement. However, he chooses to give his brain a rest during the construction of his own portfolio.

Charlie owns nine different mutual funds. He makes automatic contributions to them through a monthly allocation process. He has no idea how much he paid for the original purchase of the fund units or the unit price of each additional purchase. He does not know the total fees involved with holding each fund. He can't say whether he is currently at a profit or loss on the total position. He is not quite sure why he chose each particular fund or how to read the annual statements. He incorrectly refers to his mutual fund units as stocks. Basically, Charlie doesn't know enough to invest his way out of a wet prospectus.

However, there are a few things that Charlie does know in this area. He does know he has put away a substantial sum of money into mutual funds over the last five years. He does know he hopes, someday, he'll be able to pull more money out of the funds than he put in. He does know his personal belief that pure stocks or bonds sound much too risky and are too much trouble to learn about. He does know mutual fund companies put their fund's objectives right on the cover of their propaganda booklets; thus, the selection process is made easy. The most important thing that Charlie does know is he feels comfortable with his mutual fund investments. This feeling of comfort makes things, such as investment knowledge and independent planning, seem trivial and unnecessary. Fortunately, our national security depends on my friend Charlie's flying ability and not his investment savvy.

Guidelines for Successful Mutual Fund Investment

In the name of constructive investment knowledge, I offer some mutual fund tips. Keep in mind that you would have never heard these from me in my capacity as an institutionally subservient, retail broker.

First of all, know exactly what you are paying before you choose a particular load option. Total it up for a complete five-year period. Use five years for an estimated holding time frame, since mutual funds are definitely not quick trading instruments. Consider the percentage of load charged going in or out, combined with the amount of annual management fees. Do not forget to consider the current spread when buying or selling. It should be extremely narrow—just a few cents—before any transaction should be entered. If the fund quotes one price for buying and selling, which indicates an averaged spread, this can be an early justification for avoidance.

No legitimate sense of urgency exists with mutual funds. They are a packaged and diluted product. Their widespread allocation keeps their unit price movements on the gradual side. The broader-oriented mutual funds buy into such stocks as the Dow Jones Industrials or the S&P 500s. With these, an investor is simply buying into market momentum. As long as the buying trend continues and the Dow and other indexes keep going up, the value of these fund units should increase. If money starts leaving the market and going back to the banks, such as in times of interest rate hikes, expect to take a hit in this area.

Specialized funds concentrate their buying in such areas as natural resources. The best advice that I can give here is to stress a proliferation relativity check. If you invest in a specialized fund, when there are only ten other funds sharing the same concentration, closely monitor the emergence of new ones. If the availability of this type of specialty fund multiplies by three or more times, it's probably time to sell. The rush of buying has occurred and a natural law sell-off is pending. The smart guys will take the sure profits. Be a contrarian by nature. When the herd is selling off a certain kind of fund, look for your buying window. The same goes for when your fund is starting to run up in price. However, you'll also have to be an independent thinker, because investment firm's train their brokers to exploit the herd mentality.

There are inherent and structural disadvantages to mutual funds, especially in times of flat or fluctuating markets. A mutual fund normally maintains at least 30 different stock positions. A mutual fund's bylaws dictate no more than 5 to 10 percent of the fund's assets can be placed into one position. I would be hard pressed to find 30 great stocks at any one time, especially in a particular sector. So by design, a mutual fund can be obliged to have some stocks of questionable quality in its portfolio.

After all the previous considerations, everything else is up to the individual. Have a definite strategy in mind when making your choice. At least be able to say why you bought a particular fund. Whether your objective is growth or income, always be aware of your returns, up to any one point. Don't rely on the fund itself to tell you how well you are doing. Remember the fund manager's mastery of the fine art of self-serving interpretation. Anyone can form a valid investment strategy; some just present it in a more appealing fashion.

Understanding the Fund Concept Is the Foundation for Success

Mutual funds are here to stay and are going to be in the portfolios of most individual investors. It is crucial, for investment success, to understand the possible pitfalls of these packaged products. Ignorant and apathetic allegiance to mutual funds will introduce you to the 16th, 17th and 18th ways you lose money.

WAY #16: *When choosing an open-end mutual fund, assume the one that claims the lowest load costs, and touts the highest performance numbers, will provide the cheapest and most competent management for your money.* After all, how much could the hidden fees add up to? A person has to be a true professional to become a mutual fund manager, right? Just look at those impressive statistics.

WAY #17: *When buying a closed-end fund, take advantage of the no commission buying opportunity during the offering period.* It makes the inevitable 10 percent drop in value much easier to take a few months later.

WAY #18: *Use a mutual fund as a place to park your money.* Further purchases can be made by monthly allotments, at whatever the unit price on the first of the month. You'll enjoy that comfortable, womblike feeling from doing something that you've always been told is right. It will be like a savings account with no stated interest rate or insurance. Having an objective, understanding the investment product's structure, calculating all related fees and determining overall profit or loss are the overrated endeavors of people with too much time on their hands. Don't worry that market institutions, such as mutual fund companies, choose not to own mutual funds themselves. They are just not as smart as you.

CHAPTER 11

The Proper Care and Handling of Cold Callers and Floor Brokers

The Ways You Lose: 19

Among the various vehicles of investment influence and market propaganda, there are two that hold a unique distinction from the rest. These two special forms of advice shoot through this nation's phone lines everyday. The convenient aspect of this duo of advisory dogma is that there is no need for a subscription, a television or friends and office associates to attain investment tips. One needs only to pay the monthly phone bill to keep the line of communication open. Of these two sources of telephonic stock market guidance, the first comes to you and the second waits for you to come to it. Please welcome, for your portfolio's entertainment, the cold caller and the floor broker.

The cold call enters your home or office with the same familiar ring of any other call. It carries the adjective "cold" because this moment is the first time the two parties, on either side of the phone, have conversed together. The topic of this call differs greatly from the usual, uninvited telephonic invader. Investments for your future, financially secure horizons and the key to stock market success are the topics of discussion. The person on the dialing side of this conversation comes bearing gifts. He offers the recipient his guidance through the market jungle. As a token of good faith, he also offers a specific investment recommendation, which is currently endorsed with the full knowledge and experience of his investment firm. This cornucopia of good tidings has come to the recipient free of charge and without having to leave the comfort of the couch or desk.

If, by chance, these benevolent cold callers cannot locate you, or if you miss their ring of opportunity, you can still receive their steady doses of stock market enlightenment. The temple of investment information is open every market day. Access is granted to all who dial its telephone number. The incoming calls are routed to the designated floor broker for that day. This highly coveted position is viewed as a privilege among the firm's professional staff. Callers can receive a stock quote, a financial news update, and the house recommendation. The greatest gift to the caller is the benefit of a one-on-one, personal encounter with a genuine market professional. It's all just another way your local brokerage firm is there to assist your investment endeavors.

The cold caller and the floor broker are the front line troops of the retail division for any investment firm. Stacks of research reports, barrages of advertising and periodic news releases are not always enough to bring in the business and the desired buying power to specific stocks. The investment firm must take its message directly to the people.

Profile of the Cold Caller

While uniquely interactive and abundant, the advisory figures mentioned previously are not quite the altruistic information sources you think they are. The cold callers are in the early stages of their financial career. These sapling investment professionals are the same people who pull floor broker duty and handle the incoming calls. The responses and advice recited by these junior personnel are scripted, and the contents are completed controlled by the senior members of the firm. Their objectives dictate the subject matter recited by the front line phone troops. As with any other advisory source, the astute investor should consider the self-serving angles and ulterior motives, before acting upon any recommendation. An effective reconnaissance begins with a definitive look at the players involved.

The cold caller is a hearty breed of human being. Especially if he is carrying a Series 7 license. Every recently hatched broker spends his first 24 months of life dialing for survival. If the broker cub is not so fortunate as to inherit a client book, he knows he must join the others in the bull pen. This gathering of raw talent is given a weekly script and an unending stack of computerized leads.

Up to this point, and depending on the firm, the rookies have probably had six months of broker training. The following year is a proving period, during which they will either qualify for the next level or be catapulted out the door. The firm determines their professional fate according to three criteria. The pertinent categories are the number of new client accounts opened, the total amount of new client assets gathered, and the amount of commissions generated from these accounts. An investment firm does not evaluate its retail brokers by how well their retail clients fare in the stock market. Portfolio performance evaluations are reserved for the personnel who handle the house's and the institutional accounts.

The cold calling broker has his own order of priorities. His list has only one real entry: the amount of commissions generated. During the rookie's development period, he does not have the luxury of an established client book that automatically generates commissions. His monthly income consists of the transaction fees that he is able to generate from speaking to new people over the phone. The ultimate goal is to gather, and retain, enough clients to eventually build a genuine retail book. Until this is achieved, 300 dials a day down the lead sheet is the rookie broker's reality.

The pitch and the product can be selected by the cold caller, but the choices are limited to those on a special list. This list is near and dear to the financial interests of the firm's house account. This is another classic example of a market institution establishing a supply, and then employing the means to create a demand, in which to feed that supply at a higher value. This special list represents what the firm is currently holding in its inventory. Additional incentives are available to brokers for being loyal to the list. The designated recommendations carry the extra payout that allows the rookie to stave off starvation for another week. With that in mind, the bull pen starts each day by frantically dialing for their livelihood.

When you fill out any type of form or ever give out personal information, you will end up on a rookie broker's exclusive-individual-with-a-high-net-worth lead sheet. The stated qualifications for being included on such a list mean nothing. If you are of the human species and at one time could fog a mirror, you will eventually receive a cold call from a rookie broker. These calls will often turn into a daily occurrence. The same lead lists are circulated to a great number of bull pens.

This results in certain areas of the country receiving a barrage of calls in a concentrated period of time. The citizens of these regions will be deluged with several cold calls a day. These calls will quite often originate from distant and aggressive brokerage houses.

The rapid proliferation of cold calling operations has lead to proposals of preventative legislation. Certain states are now imposing regulations on business interests that contact prospective customers over the phone. These states will attempt to impose penalties on investment firms found to be in violation of their cold calling laws. Approval is to be obtained, in advance, from the prospective client before the receipt of an unsolicited call. This legislative trend seems to be gaining popularity.

In the face of this growing sentiment, I offer the following advice: Fight the impulse to legislate the cold calling broker out of existence. These WATTS line warriors are a tough and creative bunch. They are highly trained in the fine art of circumventing obstacles. Whether the obstacle is an objection from a prospective client or a business prohibitive, state regulation, the resourceful stock broker will find a way around it. (If you ever want to observe a living monument to overcoming adversity, spend a happy hour in a singles bar where stock brokers hang out.) Should these cold callers ever be legally prohibited from contacting prospects over the phone, they will find another way to effectively reach their prey. The new methods will probably include door-to-door assaults on selected neighborhoods or increasing the mailer barrage to epic proportions. This will not be an acceptable alternative. Preserve the cold caller's right to dial. Any unwanted call can be ended by simply hanging up the phone. It will save the wear and tear on your door's wood finish and the strain on the environment and our landfills.

Profile of the Floor Broker

The floor broker is the other personally interactive advisory source maintained by your local investment firm. The floor broker is often given the title of broker of the day. He is a cold caller whose name came up on the phone duty schedule. A shift as the floor broker isn't such a bad deal for the rookie. At least there isn't the standard screaming, moaning and groaning that occurs when dialing to the often unreceptive outside world. One prevalent downside to being the floor broker is that so many people with too much time on their hands call in to see how much of his time they can waste.

As the phones are turned on at the market's opening bell, the calls from the outside world start to hit the switchboard. Each incoming call is routed to the floor broker. Most of the individuals are calling in for a free quote or to ask about pertinent news releases flashing on the Quotron screen. There is the occasional commission from the person who is calling to set up an account to liquidate some stock. For the rookie, it is usually a small, one-time commission and a credit for opening an account. Occasionally, an individual will call in to open an account and actually buy a stock or one of the firm's packaged products. Caution must be exercised by the floor broker. There are many predators calling in to rip off the naive and hungry rookie, but that is a subject for another time. The floor broker's intended purpose is to convert the callers who are looking for general advice into new clients to buy the firm's flavor of the day.

When the caller asks for the firm's opinion of a particular stock or market sector, the floor broker quickly checks his approved inventory sheet. If the stock mentioned in the inquiry is not on the list, the floor broker must direct the callers buying interest to one of the firm's choices. He is more effective if he picks an inventory stock that is in the same market sector mentioned by the caller. The floor broker implements the clicking sounds and the standard pause, as if he is calling up valuable research on the computer. His response to the caller's question is taken from the standard script.

"Hmmm, let's see (click, click, pause). Oh, here it comes. Well, according to our latest market intelligence the particular stock that you are interested in appears quite frothy at the moment. We strongly suggest you avoid it completely. However, this morning our analyst found a stock in the same market sector on the verge of a major breakout . . ."

The floor broker can do this routine in his sleep. He realizes the majority of incoming calls are from freeloaders and freaks, but his filtering skills are very sharp. After a few seconds into the conversation, he is able to determine which callers are nontransactional wastes of time and which callers represent instant pay dirt. This skill ensures the right caliber of individuals receive the best of this unique interactive market guidance.

Whether the investor receives the broker's call or decides to the call the brokerage firm, I place the responsibility for any resulting market losses on the individual investor. Individuals make investment decisions based solely on the story being pitched through the phone line. So many clients throw their money wherever this advisory mode directs them. This commitment of funds is done without any prior consideration of the source's angle or ulterior motive. The reality of stock market mistakes and losses administers a painful enlightenment. This pain can be avoided, if the dangers of the phone borne sources of personally interactive advice are observed, before the commitment of capital.

Circumstantial Evidence of Tainted Advice

Making investment decisions based solely on tips from cold callers and floor brokers is much like choosing a date by the descriptions and phone numbers scrawled on the public bathroom wall. This is yet another example of how individuals use different decision-making criteria in their approach to the stock market than they use in the rest of their daily lives. A step back to an objective position reveals the self-imposed peril to which individuals subject themselves. Especially when they follow investment advice fraught with ulterior motive from a biased source.

Consider the advice manufacturing process and the eventual feeding to the public, through an investment firm's cold callers and floor brokers. The beneficial qualities of the offered guidance are very suspect.

Let's start with the distribution points of an investment firm's advice. When you answer the phone and realize it is a cold-calling stockbroker, you can assume a few things immediately. First, this cold-calling stockbroker is new to the business. Anyone who has ever derived their livelihood by asking people for money over the phone will confirm how unpleasant it is.

However dismal, it is a reality for almost all new stockbrokers. Bull pens are stocked with aspiring brokers who fill their days with frantic dialing. The majority of these burnout before their training is over. Three years is the maximum time period that a stock broker should still be cold calling to make a living. After this point, he is expected to meet his production goals from his established client book, referrals and inherited accounts from departing brokers.

It is quite possible that you have more stock market experience than the cold calling broker. If you listen closely, you'll be able to detect a level of frustration and desperation in his voice. It is reflective of his situation. He does not yet understand the system around him, he starts each production month at zero, he works against a draw that does not even surpass minimum wage and he has an office manager screaming at him every time the phone is not against his ear. If his call comes to you in the evening, you can bet he's been toiling away since early that morning, while wondering why he didn't get a real job after college. Above all this, he is expected to cold call you with an investment idea, which you are to accept as worthy of your venture capital.

This situation is the same for the floor broker who is a cold calling broker, pulling the duty that day. The floor broker is also among the new industry inductees. The broker-of-the-day schedule is filled by the bull pen inhabitants. The bright spot for the broker on floor duty is that he gets to pitch people who called in on their own.

It is possible for a cold caller or a floor broker to be astute in the ways of the market, even though he is new to the industry. A rookie is capable of rendering beneficial advice, but his general guidance leads to a specific recommendation. The particular investment of the day is selected by the investment firm's management. Every trade executed by a stock broker is scrutinized by the firm's supervisory staff. While a broker is employed by an investment firm, management can exercise complete control on which investments are pushed on the client base.

The Advice Rendered Can Often Serve the Best Interest of the Adviser

The investment firm should be viewed as a market competitor, vying for capital gain at everyone else's expense. How good can the investment advice of the cold caller and the floor broker possibly be? The voice on the phone is most likely that of an inexperienced person in dire straits. This rookie makes less, but works much longer than the guy who just handed you your order at the drive-through window. The broker's advisory strings are being pulled by a management team, with allegiance to the interests of the institution. And these cold callers and floor brokers bring in the bulk of the firm's retail clients.

Beyond the slanted process that creates and distributes a firm's recommendation list, individual investors should also consider who they are in the stock market transaction process. Many clients believe their investment success is the first priority of their firm. Although an investment firm does want to retain its client base, individual client satisfaction is not necessary. When the individual client decides to invest $3,000, the measly $150 gross commission is not where the firm makes its money. The big profit margins are provided by the investment banking business, the large institutional clients and the spreads and capital gains from moving the stocks in the house inventory. As always, if an individual client blows up, ten more can be found over the phone.

Be wary of any person or entity that gives you investment advice. Be aware how an investment firm makes its real profits. No firm is going to give you a hot stock tip, unless your acting upon it works in their immediate best interest. The broker is just an external tool used by the market institutions to attain their goals. The firms realize that stockbrokers come and go just like clients. Know with whom you are competing.

You might want to entertain the following tip from a relatively safe, defanged stock market snake: Take a contrarian approach to an investment firm's general and specific market advice. Let your internal cynicism direct you. This simple strategy should increase your chances of success, because it would be quite rare to see an investment firm actually follow the advice it offers.

Take a Dose of Cynicism When Listening to Cold Callers and Floor Brokers

Beware of phone calls, in either direction, bearing investment advice. The stockbrokers who diligently make the cold calls and stand the duty as the floor brokers constitute the 19th way you lose money.

WAY #19: *Take advantage of the interactive stock market advice available from your local investment firm.* Whether the informative call comes to you or you decide to call in on your own, an investment professional is standing by to administer that personal attention. Hey, why spend the time learning to make your own educated decisions? All the market guidance you could possibly need is available, in abundance, from the inside source.

CHAPTER 12

Maintaining Your Own Portfolio's House

The Ways You Lose: 20

There are certain perils that come to those with trusting souls in the investment world. There are individuals who believe the market information presented to them is designed for their benefit. There are individuals who blindly trust market professionals to operate in their best interest. These individuals also trust the brokerage firm to handle their account and their funds properly, and without any self-serving bias. This trust, boldly offered by the investing public, is not what it appears to be. The public's trust has not been granted to the stock market institutions because of excellent performance and guidance records. This issuance of trust is simply a matter of convenience. Perhaps this trust would be better classified as apathy and laziness.

In the short-term, it is much easier to trust the retail investment system and those who dwell within. This way, all that is required of the individual investor is to listen to a product pitch, write the check and hope for the best. If the individual happens to make some money and actually take the profits, then he has this special miracle to talk about in the lunchroom. If his experience is typical and he loses on the venture, he will still have something to talk about in the lunchroom. He can share his story of rapid stock value decline with his associates. His colleagues can console each other by sharing similar, personal stock market experiences.

Those who have been burned by the market can all raise a glass of port and toast to the evil that is the stock market. In unison, they can proclaim they had entered the market with honorable intentions. They trusted the system and its professionals. In the end, they were abused and their asset value was taken from them by mean people in a bad market. All of this occurred through no fault of their own.

This group's sentiment, while quite popular, rings hollow. The stock market is only as confusing and evil as an individual allows it to be. The individual investor must accept certain responsibilities when constructing a portfolio. These responsibilities include understanding the underlying principles of the market, considering the various angles and ulterior motives of those who operate in the market and choosing an investment product which fits a personally, predetermined risk-reward objective. A majority of an individual investor's losses can be attributed to bad premarket decisions, which result from shirking their personal responsibilities to their portfolio.

Investors' Responsibilities to Their Own Portfolios

The individual investor invites a bonanza of self-imposed problems, when she chooses to shirk her responsibilities as an individual investor. She joins the vast ranks of investors who send in their money and just allow things to happen to them. In the short term, she has saved time and trouble by issuing her trust, instead of acting in her own best interest. However, she will be able to use this extra time to console herself with others who have had bad market experiences.

A popular responsibility, shirked by individual investors, is properly scrutinizing advisory information. The information can be a quote or a timely buy recommendation. Investors save time and trouble by making a hasty decision, based solely on a single information source. I am not suggesting an investor should take months and consult every form of advice available, before making an investment decision. However, by not cross-checking information, investors run the risk of paying higher spreads and share prices than necessary, being influenced by false news reports and buying at the peak of a promotion and price run.

One Shirked Responsibility Can Start a Destructive Chain Reaction

Once this first responsibility has been shirked, the investor has accepted her single source of information and is now a proud share-holder of something. She now receives a monthly account statement and she shirks her second responsibility, which is to analyze it. The ability to interpret the account statement is not a priority among individual investors, especially when there is someone standing by to interpret it for them.

The customer service operator is there to render an overly objective and equally incomprehensible explanation that leaves the caller more confused than before. If the investor holds her account at a full-service brokerage firm, she can have a personal explanation from her very own stock broker. This explanation is overly subjective, but also equally incomprehensible. Especially when the broker tries to explain why the share price appears so low on the statement.

When the investor shirks her responsibility to interpret her own statement, she makes it virtually impossible to independently gauge her investment results. Her true market values, profits and losses, and interest yields become as mysterious as the statement they are printed on.

An important piece of data on the account statement that is missed by investors not possessing the skills of independent interpretation is a covert entry known as the return on assets or ROA. This particular return on assets pertains to the investment firm's own return on your assets. The amount of this entry is a year-to-date total of the fees and commissions that have been generated from your account.

The Responsibility of Vigilance

The investor has purchased her stock position and is receiving her monthly statements, while shirking two responsibilities so far. She is now ready to shirk her third responsibility. An individual investor has an obligation to herself to closely monitor the activity within her own account. She should be vigilant of what occurs and take immediate corrective action in response to out of the ordinary events.

One such event would be the appearance of a mystery trade. These mysteries occur when a new position is suddenly purchased, with cash held in the account, or with the proceeds from the sale of a current position. It's all a mystery to the investor, since she doesn't recall approving these transactions beforehand. Her lack of vigilance and her lack of immediate, subsequent action tells the abusing party a few things about her character.

The orchestrator behind this mystery trade received a covert reward for his unauthorized action. This reward usually involves much stronger incentive than the transaction commission. If the culprit is a stock broker, he must carefully choose in which accounts to place these mystery, yet covertly lucrative trades. These accounts must fit special criteria, because he doesn't want to lose the payoff should the trade have to be reversed.

He first looks for clients who don't pay much attention to their accounts. Combine that feature with a substantial cash fund balance, several obscure stock positions or a margin account with plenty of buying power, and this account has met the first stage criteria. The broker, turned bad, will start by placing a modest amount of his special stock in the account to gauge any reaction.

Should the client catch the unauthorized tester trade immediately and cry foul, the broker will quickly have the trade corrected and provide an evasive excuse for how it could have happened. If the client is not paying attention and the tester trade goes unnoticed, the broker will place another unauthorized trade in a size that reaps enough reward to justify the risk.

A deterioration of ethical standard can happen to any stock broker, even with the best intentions. He begins to see the reality of his position. He knows he must guide his accounts according to the firm's overall objectives. Whatever the inherent benefit to move a certain stock, the firm gets the major portion of the payoff and endures only minuscule risk. The broker, used as a primary tool in the process, receives a measly fraction of the gross commission and is vulnerable to repercussions from the day of the trade forward. Should the client become dissatisfied with the firm-sponsored recommendation, the broker will bear the brunt of client disgruntlement.

If the client wants to complain after buying the firm's recent recommendation, the broker will pay with mental anguish. If the client decides not to pay for the stock after the order, the broker will pay out of his own pocket. The bigger the wave of incoming client despair, the bigger the possible repercussions. When the buyer remorse over a recent firm stock pick becomes too big for the broker to handle, the issue reaches the manager in complaint form. Management will admonish the broker. True, he was supposed to move the firm's recommendation, but only into appropriate client accounts. The clients are informed, by management, that the broker was acting out-of-line and the firm will do whatever possible to correct the situation. Stock brokers know how quickly their firm will abandon them in times of trouble, regardless of seniority.

Brokers realize they are in the middle of two unfaithful entities. The firm will reap the immediate rewards of its own objective pursuits, of which the broker will share in only a small percent. However, the broker will be hung out to dry should client disgruntlement result in a monetary loss or a registered complaint toward the firm. Brokers view a good number of the client base as potential time bombs. With so many investors who do not understand the risks of the market, who are not suited for stocks or who are dishonest, the broker is the constant target of complaint and corrective action. Nevertheless, a person becomes a broker by choice and makes a conscious decision to stay or leave such a volatile environment.

For the corrupt broker who decides to stay in the industry, there are special stocks that grant him greater reward than just a commission when he places them into his client accounts. Perhaps it is covert warrants, options or cash payment under the table. He figures if he is taking all the risk by standing between the firm and the clients, he might as well take his just share of the reward. Once the potential accounts are tested, a quick and larger scale campaign is planned. The unethical broker will make a quick profit from the individual investors who shirk their responsibilities of account vigilance. This unethical behavior is never justified and erodes the very foundation of our stock market system.

The unethical broker knows the unvigilant investor can be taken for a fool. The longer it takes an investor to notice the presence of a mystery stock, the easier it is for the broker to justify its existence. This type of investor can be convinced the stock purchase had been discussed two months earlier, with a little persuasive broker rhetoric. If acceptance is not granted to the stock, this investor will usually accept any one of several lame excuses. These excuses include a lengthy time period required to correct the trade. The investor is assured the correction will be made, but the process does take a few weeks to reflect on the statement. By that time, the broker can find another qualified account in which to put the stock.

The Responsibility of Understanding a Basic Principle

A final responsibility, most often shirked by the masses, is the understanding of basic stock market principles. The stock market's unique principle of supply and demand is a very popular one to avoid learning. It is very simple: Establish a supply of a certain stock, and by whatever means necessary create the demand in which to feed that stock at a higher price. Investors do not realize they are part of the created demand when presented with promotional material and recommendations. They think their broker is buying the same stocks that he is presently touting. By not understanding basic stock market principles, such as supply and demand, the client assumes she is investing exactly as her firm invests.

The client may be investing in what her firm has purchased, but she does not receive the recommendation until long after the stock is in the firm's inventory. Once the buying interest has been created and the stock begins to move up, clients will be buying what the firm is selling. This revelation should be quite clear to anyone who has bought or followed the price charts for a firm's recommended stocks. It would be very tough for an investment firm to stay in business if its own portfolio performed as poorly in the market, as the majority of its clients' portfolios.

Guidelines for Portfolio Responsibility

The perils facing those investors who shirk their responsibilities can be avoided. Simple guidelines can be implemented to make up for previous mistakes. It is up to the individual to increase her influence on the future and fortunes of her own portfolio.

Analyzing and comprehending the monthly account statement can be simplified. The first step is to open the statement on the day it arrives. Check the account activity section for any mystery trades, while memories of the previous month are still fresh. If you paid attention to the advice that margin accounts are not appropriate for individual investors, it will be much easier to determine your true account value.

It is important to monitor the current profit and loss status of the portfolio. The regular cash account is much easier to evaluate than its margin counterpart. For all stock positions purchased with the objective of capital gain, the review should be based on total net asset value, not just by share price. The total cost of a position should always be kept in personal records and should include commissions and transaction fees. The same commissions and fees must be figured into the proposed sale of the positions. The total amount invested must always be compared against the net amount that would be realized, if the position was liquidated. It is a simple concept, but rarely followed by investors unsure of their progress in the stock market. The decision to hold or sell the position is ultimately up to the investor. It is a decision made easier by first knowing the position's net profit or loss.

Beyond the total cash in and total net cash out comparison, other numerical entries can be understood without too much effort. An inquiring phone call can supply all the necessary answers. This phone call should not be made to the broker, or even the office that handles your account. You should seek explanations from the headquarters of a national firm or the clearing company for an independent firm. You want the explanation to be objective, and there are certain statement entries that your broker might not want you to understand, such as the ROA amount mentioned earlier.

In relation to what this number signifies on the account statement, the return represents the money that has been paid to the firm from your assets. All the commissions and transaction fees, year-to-date, are listed on the unmarked ROA line. By circumventing your immediate brokerage firm and calling the more objective explanation sources, you can reveal the hidden features of your monthly account statement.

You should also avoid the perils of investing by a single source of information. Contrary to what some members of the investment industry would like the investing public to believe, you will not miss the investment opportunity of a lifetime by taking the time to cross-check the various aspects of a recommendation. Whatever the source issuing the recommendation, it is in the issuer's best interest for the recipients to respond in a timely fashion. The time-sensitive objective could be to focus buying power to move the specific stock up, to clear the specific stock out of the firm's inventory account or for the broker to make his monthly production quota. The investor can cross-check the information to help determine if the recommendation serves his best interest.

An investor should attentively listen or scrutinize a stock recommendation by phone and call the source back before making a decision. Within ten minutes, much of the vital information presented can be cross-checked. You can call another investment firm to verify the price quote, the spread and recent news releases concerning the stock. The information from both sources should match, before any further consideration is given to the original recommendation.

If you allow yourself three days to consider the merits of the information presented, you can greatly expand the scope of your scrutiny. Through an online service or even a public library, you can obtain a chart of the stock's recent price and volume history. You can also obtain a chronological listing of the news releases related to the stock. From this information, you can determine if the stock is currently trading at an usually high price and volume. You can also compare the recent news releases with past news releases and determine what effect they have had on the stock's short-term price.

In a time period of ten minutes to three days, you can avoid becoming part of the created demand that serves someone else's investment objective. The astute investor will decline to act on information that is misquoted, incorrect or recommends a purchase in the midst of a biased promotion or near the end of a production month.

The responsibility of vigilance over your account activity must be fulfilled. This is especially important if you must deal with the appearance of a mystery trade. Speed and assertiveness are key ingredients of the quick and effective remedy for an unauthorized trade. The broker should be called immediately, informed of the mystery trade, just in case he didn't know, and then ordered to correct the situation. It is possible for an unauthorized trade to occur by another broker entering the wrong account number on the buy ticket; however, it is rare. An unauthorized trade can be corrected in one day. Regardless of the cause, the broker should be able to fax you a correction confirmation by the end of the business day.

Give the broker one chance to correct the situation. Any call back from him not containing the statement of mission complete should be met with a stern warning that your next call will be to the firm's national compliance office, or to the clearing firm's headquarters, if your broker works for an independent. There isn't a stock broker in the world who wants the wrath of a branch manager recently informed of an unauthorized trade from his regional superior.

When a stock broker has had to endure the trouble and expense of a trade correction, you will probably be kept off the sucker list the next time. Whether the information that guides your investing reaches you by telephone, subscription or by second-hand conversation, it should always be cross-checked to avoid the obvious premarket mistakes.

A Tip for Constructively Curious Investment Minds

I will now offer you my most exclusive tip. This tip relates to the multitudes of investors who harbor the myth that their investments run parallel to those of their broker and brokerage firm when, following the firm's advice. When a stock broker or his firm tells you what stock to buy and when to buy it, it's a safe bet that the broker is not buying the stock at that moment. You can also bet that the broker's personal investment history, or the contents of his current portfolio, does not match the guidance he has administered to his clients. There is a simple litmus test for those who reject the notion that their brokerage firm is telling its clients to do as it says, not as it does.

Most investment firms, especially the major brokerage houses, require their retail brokers to hold their personal accounts with the firm. This means your broker's personal account information is accessible on the same computer database as his clients. This database reveals an account's current holdings, position values, cash positions and transaction history. To move between various accounts is a simple matter of entering a new account number. With this information in mind, my verification technique might seem a bit sneaky, but sneakiness is a part of stock market survival.

Call your broker and set an appointment to meet at his office. Tell him you would like to review your portfolio's previous market year. Mention you would like to plan the investments for the coming year, before depositing more money in the account. Mentioning that you will be depositing more money will inspire the broker to set the appointment at the earliest open date.

During the appointment, listen attentively to your broker's review of your account's previous activity. Your broker will have the computer screen swiveled at an angle, granting both you and he visual access. The database window he uses during this appointment will display your account's current holdings and past transactional activity. As your broker reaches the end of his review, and just before he begins to plan your investments for the coming year, make your revolutionary request. His response to this request will reveal the character of this person who is handling your investment account.

Ask your broker to call his account up on the screen. Request he show you the same window that displays his current positions and his account's past history. Observe his initial reaction to this investigative demand. His degree of talent and experience will dictate how much surprise is present on his face. However, it will be his vocal response that will convey the most information.

If he tells you he cannot access his account through this database, he is lying to you. If he tells you he doesn't have an investment account, then he is making quite a statement: He is willing to make his living with your money in the stock market, but he is not crazy enough to follow the firm's advice with the commitment of his own money. Should he refuse to call up his account on the grounds of privacy, then you have immediate justification to transfer your account. If he complies with your request and calls his account up on the screen, at least he won't attempt to insult your intelligence to your face.

When he calls up his account, examine his transaction history. See if he has purchased the same stocks that he has recommended to you. If any matches can be found between your account and his account, check the dates of his buys and sells against the times he had urged you to buy or sell the related stocks. Any discrepancies or major differences between the two accounts should be the next topic of discussion with your broker. The individual investors who conduct my exclusive verification technique will be very surprised at what they discover in their broker's account.

Risk: The Avoidable and the Inevitable

At the risk of repeating myself, I want to restate my objective:

> To provide the essential information for the individual investor, known also as the retail client, to form a mental arsenal of stock market understanding, that will protect the individual from repeating common self-victimizing mistakes.

These mistakes are committed during an individual's premarket decisions, before the funds actually enter the market. Individual investors should be able to go forth with the information presented here and deal more intelligently with their stock broker, investment firm and personal source of stock market information. The stock market is an arena in which the individual can definitely make money, but an increased understanding of the forces involved is paramount to individual success. The stock market is only as complicated as the investing public allows it to be. My informative offering is intended to build the necessary understanding and serve as a guide through the minefield set between the individual investor and the stock market.

The individual investor needs to understand the basic idea of risk. Your money, no matter how it is positioned, is always at risk. Conventional wisdom has traditionally endorsed the idea that the more money a person hopes to gain from her portfolio, the higher the risk at which her portfolio is placed. However, the depositors of certain savings and loan institutions who witnessed the sudden loss or freezing of their assets due to circumstances beyond their control would probably refute that theory.

The risk to one's money comes in four general formats: Taxation, inflation, adverse fluctuation and ignorance. Taxation and inflation are among those social events that are considered inevitable, much like coups following revolutions. How effectively people handle taxes and inflation depends on their personal choice of a CPA and their amount of creative imagination.

Adverse fluctuation is also an inevitable occurrence affecting one's monetary net worth. As the investing public's emotions and herd mentality progress through cycles, so does the drastic buying and selling trends that hit the markets. There will be times when selling pressure hits the stock market, or a specific sector or share issue, and it will be impossible to have seen it coming. Adverse market fluctuations are an inherent risk involved in the pursuit of competitive capital gains. However, even this type of inevitable risk can be diminished as people increase their commitment to understand the stock market arena.

Ignorance is the one form of monetary risk that is not inevitable. Do not allow the complicated appearance of the stock market to deter your pursuit of understanding. That is how a person falls prey to the market's unethical forces. Know what type of investment you have bought and know the related objective. Ensure that the investment and your objective match, and that the objective is being met. Have the ability to monitor and interpret the events of your own portfolio, otherwise someone else will do it for you, or to you.

It is exclusively your responsibility to maintain your own portfolio's house. To shirk this responsibility leads to the 20th way you lose money.

WAY #20: *Trust the retail investment system and the professionals who work there.* Checks and balances have been put in place to enhance your investment experiences. Investors can sleep tight, because with the abundant market information and guidance available, all that is required of them is to mail in their check and hope for the best. Think of all the time you'll save by not being informed, vigilant and cynical.

Guiding Principles To Construct Your Own Investment Strategy

As you venture in to the stock market, incorporate the following principles into your personal investment strategy:

1. Stock prices move because of overwhelming buying or selling pressure.

2. Influential market information presented to you will be tainted with self-serving bias or with the ignorance of the source.

3. Your brokerage firm should be viewed as your competitor, striving for its own profitable market returns at your expense, if necessary.

4. There are only two pure forms of financial market investment: stocks and bonds. A capital gains objective calls for a stock investment. More conservative objectives of competitive interest yield are achieved through bonds. A combination of these two objectives can be satisfied by investing in a common stock, paying a decent dividend. Beyond stocks and bonds is the realm of packaged and derivative investment products, such as mutual funds, annuities and options. By placing your money into packaged or derivative investments, you can incur the added risks of hidden fees, limited access to one's assets,

incomprehensible results due to over allocation and self-victimization through product misuse.

5. The individual investor can be as savvy and knowledgeable as any market professional who ever spoke through the phone, on the television screen or in printed matter. The individual can develop a biased market strategy that works in his or her own best interest, for a change.

6. Avoid investing with the herd. Comfort should not be found by joining the mass investment endeavors of your peers. The herd mentality is well understood and expertly exploited by those who dwell within the market jungle. If you find yourself rushing in or out of a position with the rest of the crowd, you're probably investing in the best interest of someone else.

A Few Words before We Part Company

To those who have made it to this point in the book, I would like to express my appreciation of your determined efforts. My intention has been to present this book as the best investment I have ever offered to the public. If market enlightenment and understanding has been found within these pages, then whatever price you paid for this knowledge will be returned many times over. You will now be able to avoid the common mistakes committed before your funds reach the market. These mistakes cost investors in much greater amounts than the cost of this book.

The stock market system in the United States is the benchmark of excellence for the rest of the world. Our strength as a nation, our economy and our standard of living are indebted to our free, financial market system. Within this arena, it is possible for the individual investor to succeed. The individual must understand the underlying principles and competitive nature of this arena. As you complete the final words of this book, you are already well on your way to that enlightenment.

INDEX

New
CD-ROM Money Maker Kits
from Dearborn Multimedia

Book & CD-ROM Set

A DEARBORN MONEY MAKER KIT

THE
MORTGAGE
KIT

THIRD EDITION

SELECT THE RIGHT LOAN
NEGOTIATE THE BEST TERMS
LOCK IN THE LOWEST RATE
UNDERSTAND ALL YOUR OPTIONS

THOMAS C. STEINMETZ
PHILLIP WHITT

Features:

- *25 minute video help with the author*
- *12-28 interactive printable forms per CD-ROM*
- *On-Line glossary of terms*
- *Quick-start video tutorial*
- *Interactive printable book on CD-ROM*
  (Print out sections you like for closer reading or writing notes.)

Start Enjoying Greater Financial Freedom
Triple Your Investment Portfolio
SAVE Thousands on Real Estate as a Buyer or Seller

Personal Finance

The Budget Kit
Create a Smart Budget That Saves You Time and Money

With this multimedia kit:
- Automate your expenses and cash flow
- Save your money for the things that really matter to you.
- Spot your actual spending patterns.
- Stay organized at tax time.
- Start enjoying greater financial freedom

Order No. 1800-1301
$34.95

Judy Lawrence uses her years of experience as a personal financial counselor to show how to organize a personal budget.

Investing

How To Buy Mutual Funds the Smart Way
Find Out How Easily You Can Buy Mutual Funds and Earn Profits the Smart Way

With this multimedia kit:
- Set your own goals and build your lifetime investment program
- Discover an easy way to avoid brokers' fees and reduce your expenses
- Monitor your funds with fully interactive worksheets

Order No. 1800-0701
$34.95

Stephen Littauer has been involved in the sale and marketing of financial and investment products for over 30 years.

Real Estate

The Homebuyer's Kit
Find the Right House Fast

With this multimedia kit:
- Negotiate with confidence
- Prequalify using the automated formulas to determine your best mortgage terms
- Chart your progress using the interactive home comparison forms

Order No. 1800-0401
$34.95

More than 10 million readers watch for **Edith Lank's** award-winning real estate column, *"House Calls"*.

The Mortgage Kit
Save Big $$$ When Financing Your Home

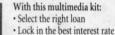

With this multimedia kit:
- Select the right loan
- Lock in the best interest rate
- Prequalify using the automated forms and checklists
- Determine how much money you will save when refinancing
- Organize your mortgage search using the interactive checklists

Order No. 1800-2201
$34.95

Thomas C. Steinmetz was a senior strategic planner with the Federal National Mortgage Association.
Phillip Whitt has worked 12 years in residential mortgage lending.

Real Estate

The Homeowner's Kit
The Homeowner's Kit Will Help You Protect Your Most Valuable Asset—Your Home!

With this multimedia kit:
- Save money and conserve energy
- Refinance for the lowest rates

Just point and click to discover:
- Hundreds of home safety and security tips
- How to inspect your home

Order No. 1800-1901
$34.95

Robert de Heer is a professional real estate author who simplifies home-owning with specific money-saving steps.

Small Business

The Business Planning Guide
Plan for Success in Your New Venture

With this multimedia kit:
- Just plug in your financials to plan your dream business
- Point and click to automate planning and financial forecasts
- Start, expand, or buy a business

Order No. 1800-0101
$34.95

David H. Bangs, Jr. is founder of Upstart Publishing Company, Inc.

Successfully Start & Manage a **NEW** Business